WEEKEND MAKES

EMBROIDERY WITH BUTTONS

25 QUICK AND EASY PROJECTS TO MAKE

WEEKEND MAKES

EMBROIDERY WITH BUTTONS

25 QUICK AND EASY PROJECTS TO MAKE

ROSEMARY DRYSDALE

First published 2024 by
Guild of Master Craftsman Publications Ltd
Castle Place, 166 High Street, Lewes,
East Sussex, BN7 1XU

ISBN 978-1-78494-645-6

Senior Project Editor: Sarah Perkins
Managing Art Editor: Darren Brant
Art Editor: Jennifer Stephens
Photography: Quail Studio
Illustrator: Fi Alexandra Hilson

Colour origination by GMC Reprographics
Printed and bound in China

CONTENTS

INTRODUCTION

I have been fascinated with buttons since I was a child. My grandfather and mother were tailors and had a sewing studio at our house, so as a child I loved playing with threads, fabrics and especially in the tins of colourful buttons. I used to sort them by colour, play counting games, make pictures, and I would imagine how they would look on pretty blouses and dresses.

Buttons have been around for centuries and were traditionally made from bone, shell, leather, wood and metal. Modern buttons tend to be made from mother of pearl, wood, resin, glass, fabric and mass-produced in plastic. They come in all shapes and sizes, and styles such as Art Deco, Vintage, Modern Art and so much more. In my collection, I have books about the history of buttons that are fascinating reads.

Most homes have a button tin or jar where odd buttons are stored. When people hold a vintage family button in their hand and remember where it was taken from, such as a special dress or a loved one's shirt, they are actually holding a piece of history.

Collecting buttons has become very popular over the years, and indeed, clubs and online groups exist for trading and comparing, as well as for selling valuable collections.

If you are beginning your own button collection, you can often find them in jars at family member's homes, at garage sales, antique shops, charity shops and local fabrics stores, to name just a few, as well as on sites such as Etsy and eBay.

Along with collecting buttons, a new trend I have been noticing is 'button art', and Pinterest and Etsy have lots of ideas for things to make with buttons, both old and new.

I've been embroidering professionally all my life, and adding buttons to embroidery is something I have explored over the years. They work so beautifully together. I hope you enjoy creating these embroidery and button designs. Feel free to experiment with your own special buttons, choosing sizes close to mine, but maybe changing the colours based on what you have found.

Have fun, be creative and watch out, you may become a collector too!

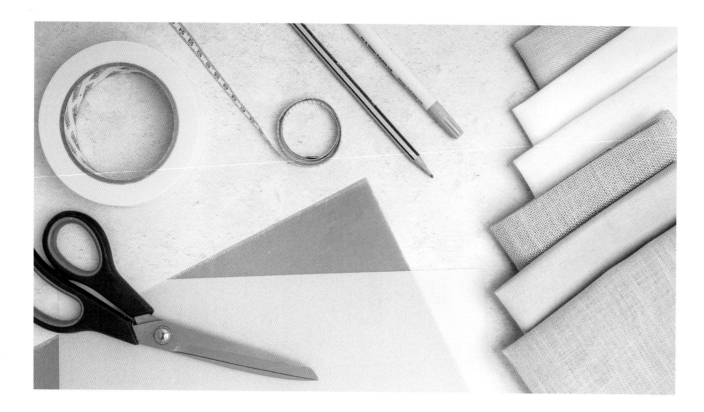

TOOLS AND MATERIALS

Before starting a project, you'll need to gather some essential items together. If you are a sewer, you probably already have some of the basic tools on hand. The fabrics, threads, buttons and embroidery hoops you'll need are readily available at craft and fabric shops, and generally quite affordable.

NEEDLES

Always use a good-quality needle with an eye large enough to allow the thread to slide easily through it. Too small an eye will cause the thread to fray and will be difficult to thread, while too large an eye may leave big holes in the fabric.

- **Embroidery Needles**: They have a fine, sharp point that easily pierces the fabric and come in a variety of sizes ranging from 1 to 10. The higher the number, the finer the needle.

Embroidery needles have a large eye to make threading easier. Do not leave the needle in the work when you are not embroidering as it can leave a mark.

- **Beading Needles**: For sewing on very tiny buttons, you may use a beading needle. They have a smaller eye and are very fine so they can fit easily through the button's hole. Beading needles also come in various sizes. Choose the size you need to fit the button you are using.

SCISSORS

It's essential to have a high quality pair of embroidery scissors to ensure clean cuts every time.

- A sharp pointed pair of small embroidery scissors with narrow blades.

- A large pair of fabric scissors used only for cutting fabric.

FABRICS

The choice of fabric is key to how your finished project comes out. Always use the best quality fabric available and choose only natural fibres such as linen or cotton. I prefer linen for its lasting qualities and ease of stitching. Most of the pieces in this book are worked on a high-quality, tightly woven linen or a good-quality cotton.

When stretched in the hoop, the fabric should be firm enough to embroider on without puckering or fraying. Avoid loosely woven or nubby fabrics as the design may not transfer completely and the stitches may not lie flat or even. For the projects using felt, choose a high-quality felt. To be sure you have chosen the appropriate fabric, you may want to try a few embroidery stitches on a scrap of the fabric you are going to use to see how they work. Your local craft store may be able to help you choose a fabric if you are unsure.

THREADS

Embroidery threads are available in an array of beautiful colours. For the projects in this book, I've provided colour options in DMC thread. I've used either stranded embroidery cotton, also known as floss, or pearl cotton (perle cotton).

Stranded embroidery floss is a divisible thread made up of six individual strands of mercerized cotton that can be separated into single strands, which then can be used as one, two, three or more strands held together to achieve different effects. For most of these projects I used three strands. If different, it's indicated in the pattern instructions.

To separate the strands from the skein, cut an 18in (45cm) length of thread from the skein, hold the thread at the top and pull the threads out one by one upwards to avoid tangling, then place the threads back together side by side before threading into the needle. A longer thread will tangle and knot. You may be tempted to use a longer thread, but 18in (45cm) is perfect.

Pearl cotton is a non-divisible embroidery cotton with a tight twist and a beautiful sheen. It comes in skeins or balls and is only used as a single thread. There are three different sizes available: size 3, 5 or 8. Size 3 is the thickest.

Note: Each skein or ball of thread has its own colour number and I have listed the colour numbers used for each project. If the suggested thread colour is not available, choose a shade as close as possible to my recommended choice.

HOOPS

Embroidery hoops come in a wide range of sizes, shapes and materials. They keep the fabric taut and flat as you are working on it, so you can keep your stitches even. In this book, we are also using them as frames to display the finished pieces.

A hoop consists of two removable rings held firmly together by a metal screw, which is used to tighten the hoop when the fabric is in place.

I use wooden hoops for my embroideries, but you can find them in metal and various shades of plastic. They come in sizes from small to large, and round, oval, square or rectangle shapes. Round hoops are the most popular and are what I've chosen for the projects in this book.

YOU WILL ALSO NEED

- Ruler or tape measure
- Ironing board and iron
- Sewing thread for basting
- Pencil
- Water-soluble pen
- Dressmakers carbon paper
- Tracing paper

BUTTONS

You can use buttons you have to hand or purchase new ones. I've indicated what sizes I used, but play around with colours, sizes and shapes to customize your design. The templates in this book show the button sizes I used. Use these as a guide – the best way is to photocopy the templates, then place the buttons on top until you are happy with the sizes and composition. This will ensure you have chosen the sizes closest to what I used.

HOW TO ATTACH A BUTTON

1. Thread your needle and tie a knot at one end.

2. Hold your button flat onto your work and bring the needle up from the back of your work, passing through one of the holes in the placed button.

3. Take your needle and thread back down through the other button hole.

4. Repeat this process four or five times to ensure the button is securely attached. Fasten off the thread on the wrong side of your work.

5. For a four-hole button, repeat step 1 and 2, but take your needle back down diagonally across the button. Repeat this again to form a cross shape.

EMBROIDERY BASICS

Whether you are brand new to embroidery or have some experience, these key steps will help you create display-ready projects to gift or keep.

GETTING STARTED

HOW TO TRANSFER A DESIGN

To transfer the drawing onto the fabric, you will need a firm surface to work on such as a board or table.

1. First trace the line drawing from the page onto the tracing paper. Lay the fabric (A) onto the hard surface and tape flat.

2. Next put the carbon paper, coloured side down (B), over the fabric, centring the traced design (C) on top. Tape it down to secure. Using the pencil, trace around the line drawing, pressing hard. Check at a corner to make sure the design is transferring onto the fabric.

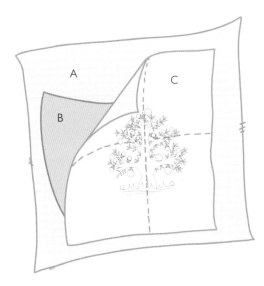

HOW TO TRANSFER A DESIGN ONTO FELT

1. Carbon Paper: See how to transfer a design using carbon paper (see left). Use white or yellow carbon paper when working on dark felt.

2. Stitching Through Paper: You will need thin paper such as tissue paper or wax paper. First trace the design onto the thin paper. Securely baste (sew on using sewing thread and large stitches) or pin the paper pattern onto the felt. Stitch your embroidery stitches through the paper onto the fabrics using small stitches where possible. When all the stitching is complete, carefully tear away the paper. You may need to use tweezers to remove any small pieces of paper remaining on the felt.

3. Iron-on Transfer Pencil: First trace the design onto tracing paper. Turn the paper over and place it on a plain hard surface, so you can see the design clearly. Draw over the design again on the wrong side using the transfer pencil. Place the design onto the fabric transfer pencil side down. Pin in place. Using a high heat setting on the iron, press for 5–10 seconds. Without removing the design, check a corner to see if the design has transferred to the felt. Press again if necessary.

4. Printable Dissolving Paper: Use stick and stitch paper or similar products available from craft stores.

PUTTING THE FABRIC IN THE HOOP

After transferring the design onto the fabric, you are ready to place it into the hoop.

1. First loosen the metal screw on the hoop. You will now have two rings: a smaller inner ring and a slightly larger outer ring. Place the inner ring under the fabric, centring the design. The drawing will be facing you.

2. Push the outer ring over the inner ring, keeping the screw at the top of the hoop. Tighten the screw, pulling the edges of the fabric a little to get the fabric taut. When the design is centred, you are ready to stitch.

FINISHING

When you're done stitching your piece, take the time to finish it neatly so it's beautiful on both sides. I've done what is called a gathered finish.

1. With a long length of pearl cotton and the wrong side facing, insert the needle into the fabric about ½in (13mm) from the outer edge of the hoop. Work a circle of running stitches (see page 18) around the perimeter of the hoop. Leave a long tail.

2. Using embroidery scissors, trim off excess fabric at least ½in (13mm) away from the running stitches. Gather the running stitches by pulling the pearl cotton thread until the fabric fits snugly around the inner hoop, then secure the thread with a few double stitches.

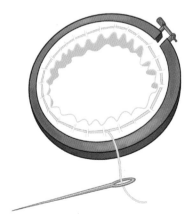

3. Place the felt backing on top of the fabric and, using pearl cotton, stitch through both the felt and fabric to attach the backing.

EMBROIDERY STITCHES

STARTING A STITCH

To begin a stitch, we use an 'away knot' on the front of the work. Tie a knot at the end of the thread you are working with and take the needle down through the front of the fabric to the back, about 3–5in (7.5–12.5cm) 'away' from where your first stitch is to begin. A long thread will be secured on the back of the work. After the stitch is completed, cut off the knot from the front of the work and thread the long thread onto the needle and weave it securely under the stitches on the back of the embroidery.

ENDING A STITCH

Take the thread to the wrong side of your work and weave it under the worked stitches for about 2in (5cm). Try to keep the wrong side of your work as neat as possible.

STRAIGHT STITCH

One of the most basic stitches, it can be worked long or short, evenly or different lengths.

Bring needle up through at A and down at B. Pull tightly enough that there is no gap, but not so tight that the fabric puckers.

RUNNING STITCH

If you know how to hand sew at all, you know how to do a running stitch!

Working from right to left, bring the needle up at A, go in at B and come back out at C. Continue in this manner, spacing stitches evenly. To end the stitch, go down through the fabric to the wrong side at B.

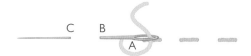

BACK STITCH

This utilitarian stitch can be used for outlines, or anywhere you need to 'draw' with thread.

Working from right to left, bring the needle up at A and make a small backwards stitch by going down at B. Bring the needle through at C. Move the needle to the left under the fabric. Continue this pattern, bringing the needle up a space ahead and down into the hole made by the last stitch. To end the stitch, go down through the fabric to the wrong side at A.

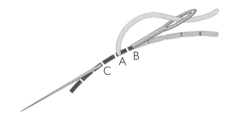

STEM STITCH

Stem stitch is most often used to make straight or curved lines, or as a filling stitch. The thread can be held to the left of needle, as shown, or to the right. Use shorter stitches when working curved lines. Keep the thread on the outside of a curve.

1. Bring the needle up at A, down at B and back up again at C. Draw the thread through and hold to the left of the needle.

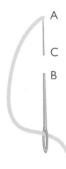

2. Bring the needle down at D and up again at B.

3. Continue Step 2, holding the thread the same side of the needle. To end the stitch, go down through the fabric to the wrong side at D.

CHAIN STITCH

Chain stitch is one of the most versatile stitches. It's basically a series, or chain, of loops. It can be used as an outline or filler. Single chain stitches are often used individually or to make flower petals, sometimes called lazy daisy. Zigzag chain stitch uses chain stitches worked at an angle to create a zigzag effect.

1. Bring the needle through the fabric at A. Form a loop and hold down with your thumb or finger. Insert the needle at A again and come back through the fabric at B. Gently pull the thread through to form the first chain.

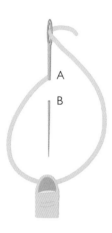

2. Repeat Step 1, always inserting the needle where the thread came out, drawing it through tightly enough to lay flat, but not so tight that the fabric puckers.

SINGLE CHAIN

Follow step 1 for chain stitch. Go down through the fabric at C, tacking the top of the stitch down. To end the stitch, go down to the wrong side of the fabric at C. Fasten off or continue to form your next single chain stitch.

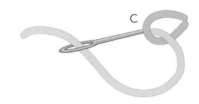

FRENCH KNOT

A favourite stitch of embroiderers, the French knot can be used as an individual element, like an eye, scattered about randomly, or used to fill in an entire area to create texture. The basic French knot is wrapped once, but you can wrap it twice, three or even four times to create a larger knot.

1. Bring the needle up at A and twist through the thread to bring it over the needle.

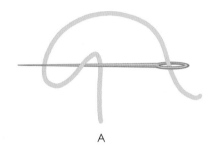

2. Pull the needle up over the thread and back down into A.

3. You are essentially tying a knot with the needle and thread. For a French knot wrapped twice, twist the thread over the needle twice in Step 1.

FISHBONE STITCH

Fishbone can be worked placing stitches right next to each other or spaced out for a more open look. It's worked off a centre line.

1. Bring the needle up at A, at the centre point of the shape, and down at B, below it on the centre line. Bring the thread up at C, just to the left of A following the outline of your shape.

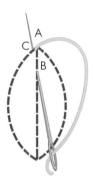

2. Bring the needle down at D, keeping the thread under the needle, forming a loop and drawing through.

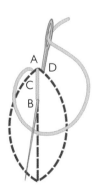

3. Bring the needle down at E, right below B and come up at F.

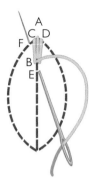

4. Continue forming loops and tying down with small, straight stitches. To end the stitch, go down through the fabric to the wrong side at E.

5. Finished fishbone effect.

FLY STITCH

This Y-shaped stitch works well for leaves and foliage.

1. Bring the needle up at A and insert the needle at B, to the right of A. Pull the needle out at C, bringing the tip of the needle over the thread.

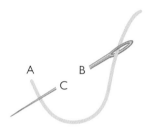

2. Pull the needle through the fabric, looping it over the stitch, pulling it down at D to form a Y-shape.

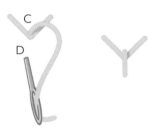

3. Continue in this way to form a neat vertical row.

SATIN STITCH

Satin stitch is a wonderful way to fill in small shapes. Working at a slight angle is much easier than straight across or up and down. For more dimension, you can use a padded satin stitch, where you can work the base row at a different angle.

1. Outline the area you want to fill with stem stitch or back stitch.

2. Beginning at the centre of the area you want to fill in, bring the needle up through the front of the fabric at A and down at B.

3. Bring the needle up through C, staying as close to the first stitch as possible.

4. Continue with this stitch until the area is filled. To end the stitch, go down through the fabric to the wrong side at B.

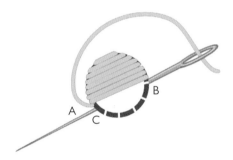

BLANKET STITCH (WORKED OVER A RAW EDGE)

This is a fun and versatile stitch that instantly adds a finished, vintage look to a piece. Stitches can be made close together for a solid look or spaced out for a more open effect.

1. Bring the needle up ¼in (6mm) from the raw edge, take the needle over the raw edge and back up where you came out. Pass the needle under the loop you just made, this creates an anchor. Move along and insert the needle in at A and bring the needle out from under the raw edge (B), holding the thread under the needle. Draw through.

2. Repeat Step 1, spacing the stitches evenly.

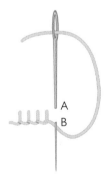

3. To end the stitching, loop through the first stitch and end off the thread on the wrong side.

PROJECTS

MINI WREATH HOOP

This simple design uses only one size button and three basic embroidery stitches, making it great for the beginner stitcher. You could change the colours to reds and greens for a holiday themed wreath.

SKILL LEVEL: EASY

YOU'LL NEED

FABRIC
- 7in (18cm) square of white linen
- 2¾in (7cm) circle of white felt for backing

HOOP
- 3in (8cm) embroidery hoop

HABERDASHERY
- Buttons (8)
  8 purple buttons, size ⁵⁄₁₆in (8mm)

- Thread
  DMC embroidery floss, 1 skein each:
  Green 320
  Pink 3833
  Purple 30

- Thread for finishing
  DMC pearl cotton 5, white

- Embroidery needle, size 6

- Dressmakers carbon paper for tracing

- Pencil

- Scissors

PREPARATION

Transfer the design onto the linen fabric (see page 14). Centre the hoop over the design, assembling it securely (see page 15).

STITCHES USED

See embroidery stitches on pages 18–23

- French knot
- Stem stitch
- Single chain stitch
- Straight stitch

METHOD

Use three strands of floss for all embroidery except for French knots, which need four strands. Work all the embroidery first, following the photo. Sew on the buttons using two strands of floss and following the photo for placement.

FINISHING

See instructions on page 16 for finishing your project and attaching the felt backing.

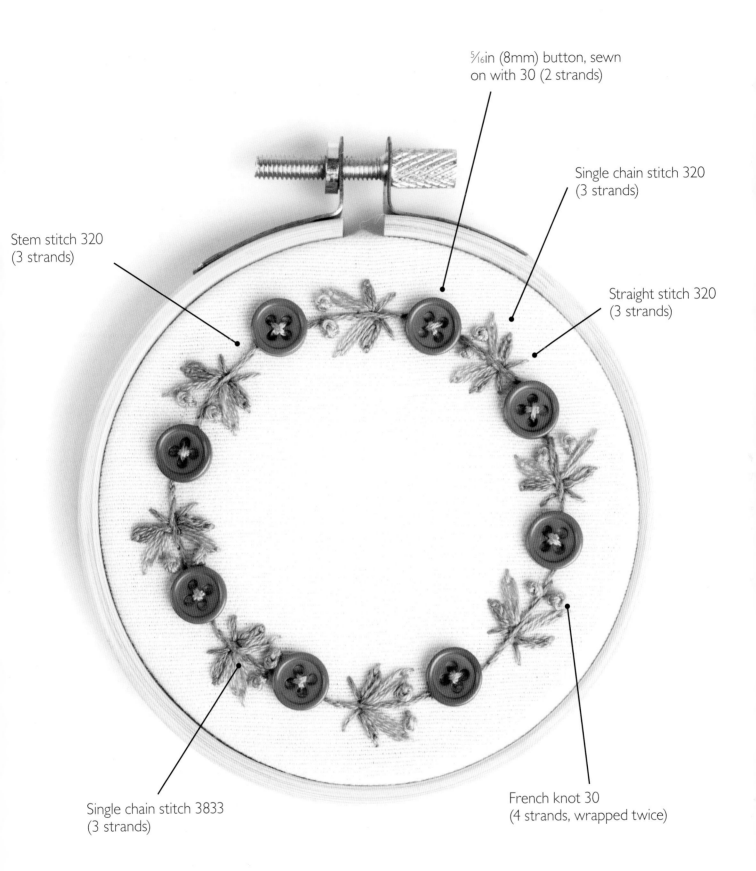

⁵⁄₁₆in (8mm) button, sewn on with 30 (2 strands)

Single chain stitch 320 (3 strands)

Straight stitch 320 (3 strands)

Stem stitch 320 (3 strands)

Single chain stitch 3833 (3 strands)

French knot 30 (4 strands, wrapped twice)

SCANDI-INSPIRED FLOWERS

These whimsical flowers are reminiscent of the folkloric flowers that have a long tradition in Swedish embroidery. A variation is to change the buttons to white with yellow button centres on a background of blue.

SKILL LEVEL: SOME EXPERIENCE

YOU'LL NEED

FABRIC
- 10in (25cm) square of white linen
- 5¾in (14.5cm) circle of white felt for backing

HOOP
- 6in (15cm) embroidery hoop

HABERDASHERY
- Buttons (29)
    12 red buttons, size ⅜in (9mm)
    6 green buttons, size ⅜in (9mm)
    3 light orange buttons, size ⁵⁄₁₆in (8mm)
    8 orange buttons, size ¼in (6mm)

- Thread
    DMC embroidery floss, 1 skein each:
    Green 911
    Orange 741
    Red 666
    Yellow 725

- Thread for finishing
    DMC pearl cotton 5, white

- Embroidery needle, size 6

- Dressmakers carbon paper for tracing

- Pencil

- Scissors

PREPARATION

Transfer the design onto the linen fabric
(see page 14). Centre the hoop over the
design, assembling it securely (see page 15).

STITCHES USED

See embroidery stitches on pages 18–23

- Back stitch

- French knot

- Straight stitch

METHOD

Use three strands of floss. Work all the
embroidery first, except for the straight stitches
and French knots between the buttons. Sew
on the buttons using two strands of floss
and following the photo for placement. Fill in
between the buttons with straight stitches and
French knots, using the photo as a guide.

FINISHING

See instructions on page 16 for finishing your
project and attaching the felt backing.

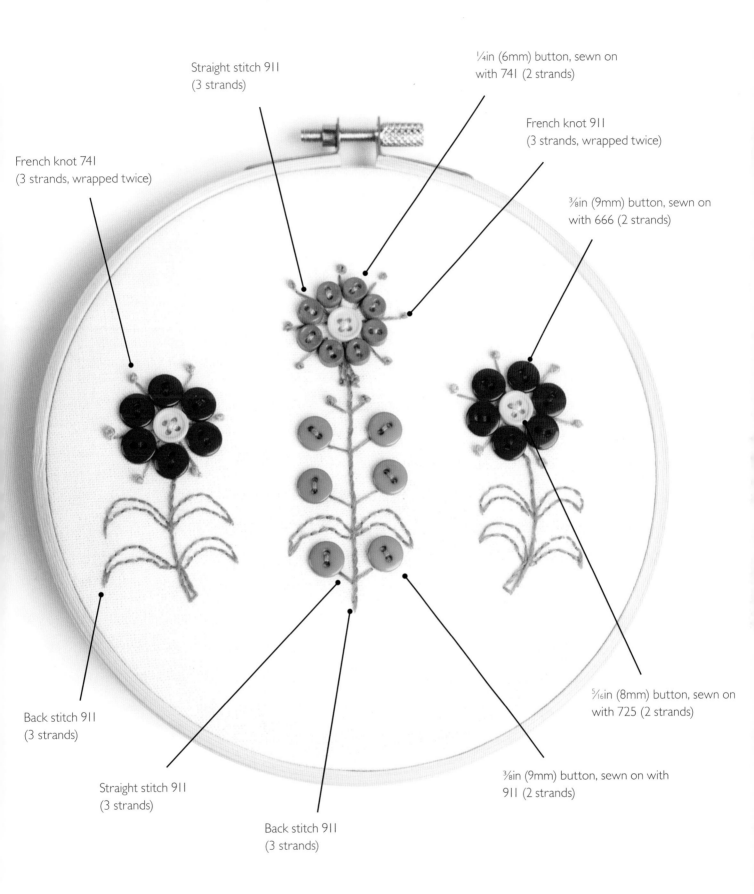

Straight stitch 911
(3 strands)

¼in (6mm) button, sewn on
with 741 (2 strands)

French knot 911
(3 strands, wrapped twice)

French knot 741
(3 strands, wrapped twice)

⅜in (9mm) button, sewn on
with 666 (2 strands)

Back stitch 911
(3 strands)

Straight stitch 911
(3 strands)

Back stitch 911
(3 strands)

⅜in (9mm) button, sewn on with
911 (2 strands)

⁵⁄₁₆in (8mm) button, sewn on
with 725 (2 strands)

OH, CHRISTMAS TREE

Inspired by feathery Scandinavian Christmas trees, this button-adorned tree is whimsically covered in snowflakes. Tiny iridescent buttons and metallic threads could give the effect of shiny Christmas ornaments.

SKILL LEVEL: SOME EXPERIENCE

YOU'LL NEED

FABRIC
* 10in (25cm) square of blue linen
* 5¾in (14.5cm) circle of white felt for backing

HOOP
* 6in (15cm) embroidery hoop

HABERDASHERY
* Buttons (12)
    1 yellow star-shaped button, size 1in (2.5cm)
    11 red buttons, size ⅜in (9mm)

* Thread
    DMC embroidery floss, 1 skein each:
    Green 703
    Red 666
    White 27

* Thread for finishing
    DMC pearl cotton 5, white

* Embroidery needle, size 6

* Dressmakers carbon paper for tracing

* Pencil

* Scissors

PREPARATION

Transfer the design onto the linen fabric (see page 14). Centre the hoop over the design, assembling it securely (see page 15).

STITCHES USED

See embroidery stitches on pages 18–23

- French knot
- Straight stitch
- Stem stitch

METHOD

Use three strands of floss for all the embroidery except for the French knots, which need six strands. Work all the embroidery first, following the photo. Sew on the buttons using two strands of floss and following the photo for placement.

FINISHING

See instructions on page 16 for finishing your project and attaching the felt backing.

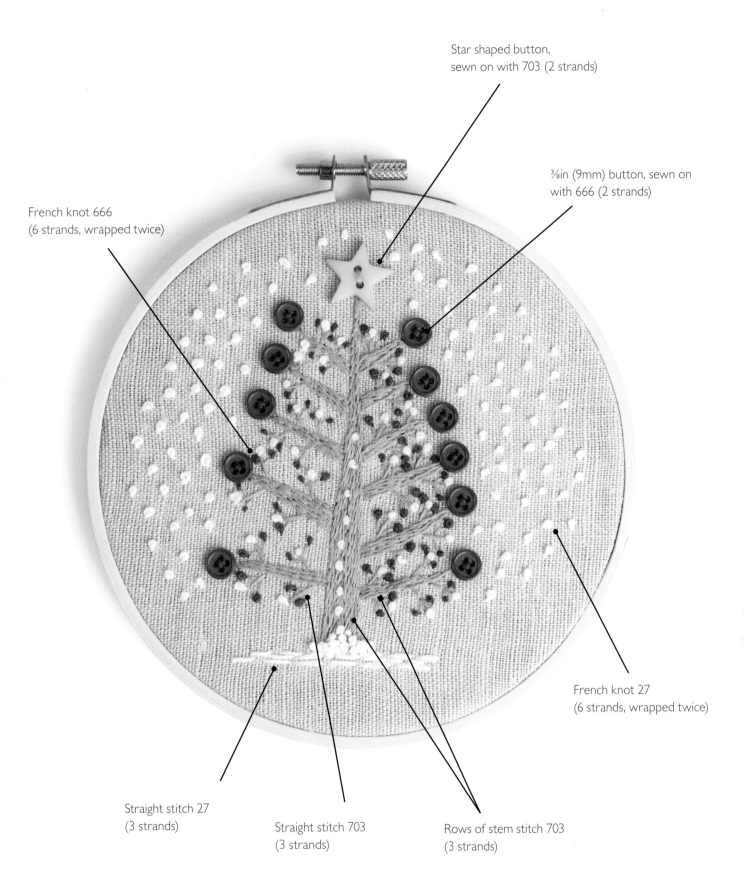

Star shaped button,
sewn on with 703 (2 strands)

⅜in (9mm) button, sewn on
with 666 (2 strands)

French knot 666
(6 strands, wrapped twice)

French knot 27
(6 strands, wrapped twice)

Straight stitch 27
(3 strands)

Straight stitch 703
(3 strands)

Rows of stem stitch 703
(3 strands)

MANDALA

This beginner project is wonderful for using up leftover buttons and playing with different colour combinations. Simple single chains and French knots add to the patterning. For a more festive effect, change the white background to a bright shade of pink or orange.

SKILL LEVEL: EASY

YOU'LL NEED

FABRIC
- 9in (23cm) square of white linen
- 4¾in (12cm) circle of white felt for backing

HOOP
- 5in (13cm) embroidery hoop

HABERDASHERY
- Buttons (33)
    1 yellow button, size ½in (13mm)
    8 blue buttons, size ½in (13mm)
    8 green buttons, size ¼in (6mm)
    12 purple buttons, size ¼in (6mm)
    4 yellow buttons, size ¼in (6mm)

- Thread
    DMC embroidery floss, 1 skein each:
    Purple 32
    Turquoise 958
    Yellow 743

- Thread for finishing
    DMC pearl cotton 5, white

- Embroidery needle, size 6
- Dressmakers carbon paper for tracing
- Pencil
- Scissors

PREPARATION

Transfer the design onto the linen fabric
(see page 14). Centre the hoop over the
design, assembling it securely (see page 15).

STITCHES USED

See embroidery stitches on pages 18–23

- French knot
- Single chain stitch

METHOD

Using two strands of floss, sew the buttons
on first and then work the embroidery using
three strands of floss for the single chain and six
strands for the French knots.

FINISHING

See instructions on page 16 for finishing your
project and attaching the felt backing.

½in (13mm) button, sewn on
with 958 (2 strands)

Single chain stitch 958
(2 strands)

¼in (6mm) button, sewn on
with 743 (2 strands)

French knot 743
(6 strands, wrapped twice)

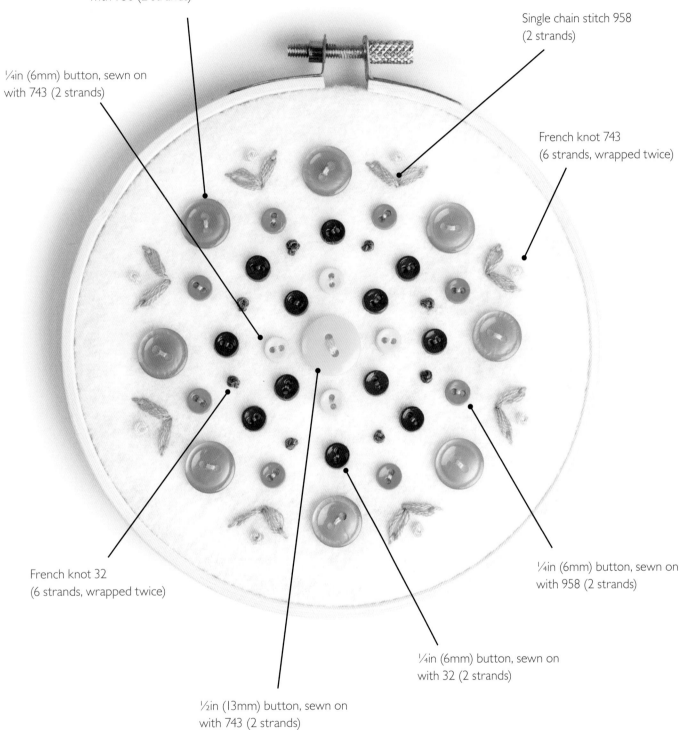

French knot 32
(6 strands, wrapped twice)

¼in (6mm) button, sewn on
with 958 (2 strands)

¼in (6mm) button, sewn on
with 32 (2 strands)

½in (13mm) button, sewn on
with 743 (2 strands)

MONARCH BUTTERFLY

Outlined with stem stitch and filled in with French knots, this stunning butterfly can be filled with a variety of button colours. It would work well stitched onto a shirt, bag or a pair of jeans.

SKILL LEVEL: EXPERIENCED

YOU'LL NEED

FABRIC
- 10in (25cm) square of white linen
- 5¼in (14.5cm) circle of white felt for backing

HOOP
- 6in (15cm) embroidery hoop

HABERDASHERY
- Buttons (54)
    2 yellow buttons, size ¾in (19mm)
    4 orange buttons, size ½in (13mm)
    2 yellow buttons, size ½in (13mm)
    4 yellow buttons, size ⅜in (10mm)
    9 yellow buttons, size ⅜in (9mm)
    10 orange buttons, size ⅜in (9mm)
    10 white buttons, size ⁵⁄₁₆in (8mm)
    1 orange button, size ⁵⁄₁₆in (8mm)
    8 orange buttons, size ¼in (6mm)
    4 yellow buttons, size ¼in (6mm)

- Thread
    DMC embroidery floss, 1 skein each:
    Black 310
    Orange 720
    White 27

    DMC pearl cotton 5:
    Black 310
    Orange 946
    Yellow 972

- Thread for finishing
    DMC pearl cotton 5, white

- Embroidery needle, size 6

- Dressmakers carbon paper for tracing

- Pencil

- Scissors

PREPARATION

Transfer the design onto the linen fabric (see page 14). Centre the hoop over the design, assembling it securely (see page 15).

STITCHES USED

See embroidery stitches on pages 18–23

- French knot
- Back stitch
- Satin stitch
- Stem stitch

METHOD

First outline the butterfly with stem stitch using three strands of black floss, then work the body in satin stitch, also using three strands. Next sew on the buttons using two strands of floss and fill in any spaces with French knots using six strands of pearl cotton, following the photo for placement.

FINISHING

See instructions on page 16 for finishing your project and attaching the felt backing.

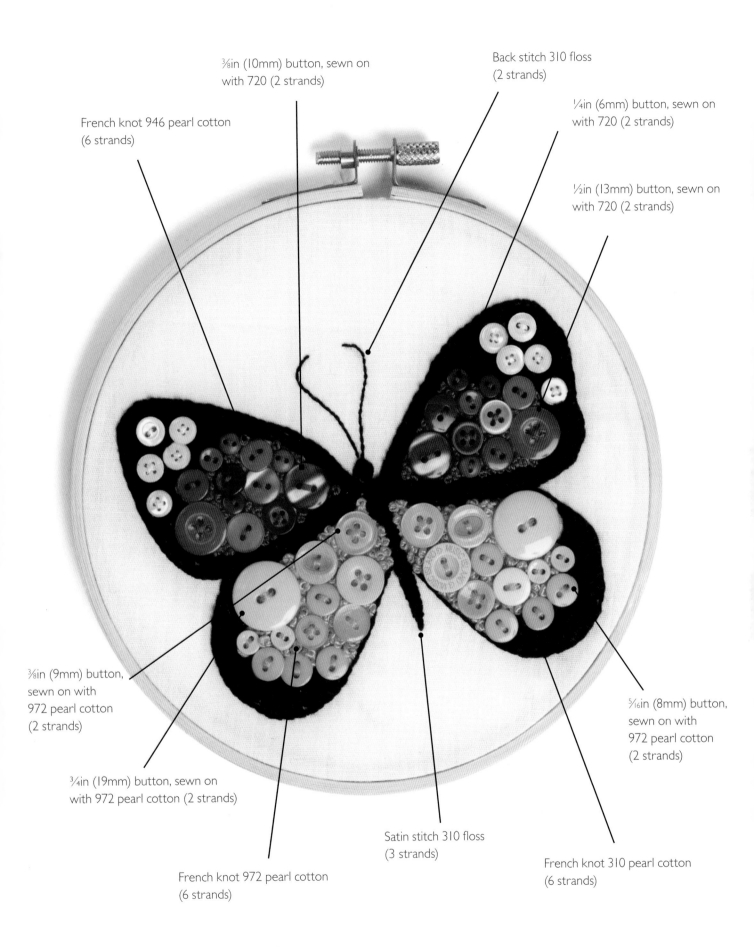

⅜in (10mm) button, sewn on with 720 (2 strands)

Back stitch 310 floss (2 strands)

French knot 946 pearl cotton (6 strands)

¼in (6mm) button, sewn on with 720 (2 strands)

½in (13mm) button, sewn on with 720 (2 strands)

⅜in (9mm) button, sewn on with 972 pearl cotton (2 strands)

⁵⁄₁₆in (8mm) button, sewn on with 972 pearl cotton (2 strands)

¾in (19mm) button, sewn on with 972 pearl cotton (2 strands)

Satin stitch 310 floss (3 strands)

French knot 972 pearl cotton (6 strands)

French knot 310 pearl cotton (6 strands)

QUEEN ANNE'S LACE

This is one of my favourite wild flowers that blooms in the garden every spring. A mixture of pearl and white buttons makes it easy to create on a sage linen background.

SKILL LEVEL: MEDIUM

YOU'LL NEED

FABRIC
- 12in (30cm) square of sage linen
- 6¾in (17cm) circle of white felt for backing

HOOP
- 7in (18cm) embroidery hoop

HABERDASHERY
- Buttons (47)
    1 white button, size ½in (13mm)
    16 white buttons, size ⅜in (10mm)
    30 white buttons, size ⁵⁄₁₆in (8mm)

- Thread
    DMC embroidery floss, 1 skein each:
    Dark green 561
    Light green 563
    White 27

- Thread for finishing
    DMC pearl cotton 5, white

- Embroidery needle, size 6

- Dressmakers carbon paper for tracing

- Pencil

- Scissors

PREPARATION

Transfer the design onto the linen fabric (see page 14). Centre the hoop over the design, assembling it securely (see page 15).

STITCHES USED

See embroidery stitches on pages 18–23

- Back stitch
- Stem stitch
- Single chain stitch

METHOD

Use floss to work all the embroidery first following the photo. Sew on the buttons using two strands of floss following the photo for placement.

FINISHING

See instructions on page 16 for finishing your project and attaching the felt backing.

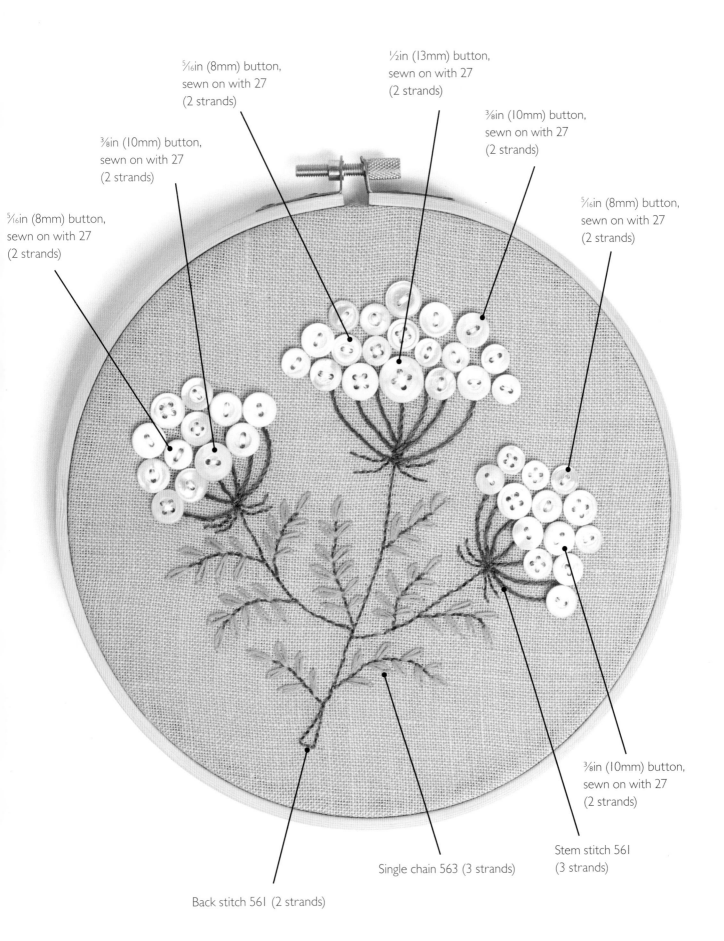

⅝₁₆in (8mm) button,
sewn on with 27
(2 strands)

⅜in (10mm) button,
sewn on with 27
(2 strands)

⁵⁄₁₆in (8mm) button,
sewn on with 27
(2 strands)

½in (13mm) button,
sewn on with 27
(2 strands)

⅜in (10mm) button,
sewn on with 27
(2 strands)

⁵⁄₁₆in (8mm) button,
sewn on with 27
(2 strands)

⅜in (10mm) button,
sewn on with 27
(2 strands)

Stem stitch 561
(3 strands)

Single chain 563 (3 strands)

Back stitch 561 (2 strands)

FELT MANDALA

Layers of felt make this a dimensional background that's perfect for adding buttons and texture with pearl cotton. I used a vintage button from my collection for the centre.

SKILL LEVEL: EASY

YOU'LL NEED

FABRIC
- 8 in (30cm) square of peacock blue felt
- 3¾in (9.5cm) circle of white felt for backing
- 2½in (6.3cm) circle of white felt
- 2in (5cm) circle of peacock blue felt

HOOP
- 4in (10cm) embroidery hoop

HABERDASHERY
- Buttons (13)
  1 large fancy vintage button for the centre, size 1in (25mm)
  6 small white buttons, size ½in (13mm)
  6 tiny turquoise buttons, size ¼in (6mm)

- Small piece of ribbon for the hanging loop

- Thread
  DMC pearl cotton 5, 1 skein each:
  Dark purple 552
  Green 907
  Purple 209
  White 27

- Thread for finishing
  DMC pearl cotton 5, white

- Embroidery needle, size 6

- Dressmakers carbon paper for tracing

- Pencil

- Scissors

- Basting thread

PREPARATION

Transfer the design onto the felt square
(see page 14). Centre the hoop over the
design, assembling it securely (see page 15).

STITCHES USED

See embroidery stitches on pages 18–23

- French knot
- Straight stitch
- Single chain stitch

METHOD

Baste the blue and white felt circles in the
centre of the hoop (see photograph). Sew
on the large white vintage button using green
thread following the photo for placement. Next,
work the embroidery using one strand of pearl
cotton. Sew on the buttons using purple thread
following the photo for placement.

FINISHING

See instructions on page 16 for finishing your
project and attaching the felt backing. Make a
ribbon loop to hang your project.

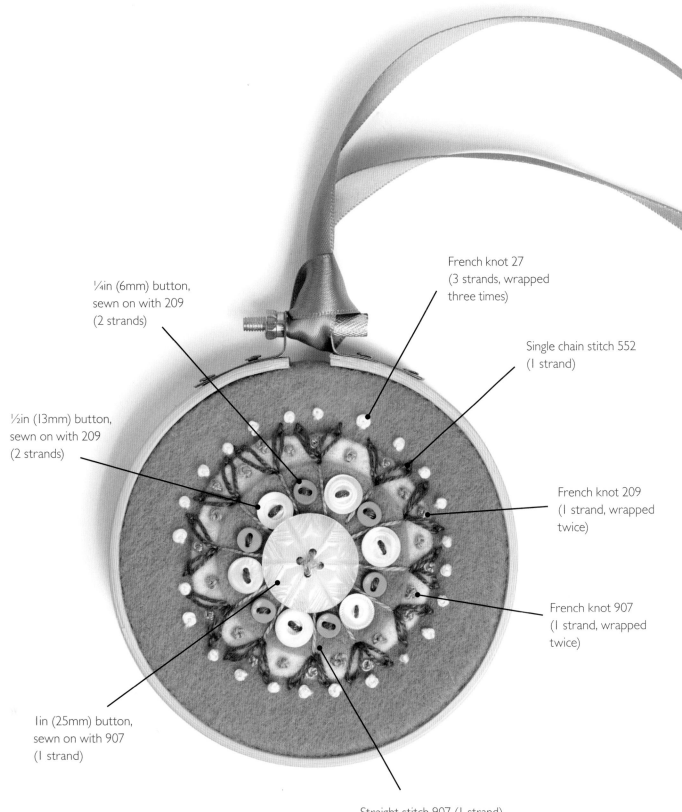

¼in (6mm) button, sewn on with 209 (2 strands)

½in (13mm) button, sewn on with 209 (2 strands)

French knot 27 (3 strands, wrapped three times)

Single chain stitch 552 (1 strand)

French knot 209 (1 strand, wrapped twice)

French knot 907 (1 strand, wrapped twice)

1in (25mm) button, sewn on with 907 (1 strand)

Straight stitch 907 (1 strand)

COCKTAIL TIME

A refreshing martini and two glasses of red wine are perfect for happy hour. Instead of displaying this in a hoop, you can place it in a window card or on the corner of a napkin.

SKILL LEVEL: EASY

YOU'LL NEED

FABRIC
- 8in (20cm) square of white linen
- 3¾in (9.5cm) circle of white felt for backing

HOOP
- 4in (10cm) embroidery hoop

HABERDASHERY
- Buttons (30)
    - 3 tiny green buttons, size ¼in (6mm)
    - 12 red buttons, size ¼in (6mm)
    - 15 white clear buttons, size ⅛in (3mm)

- Thread
    - DMC embroidery floss, 1 skein each:
    - Grey 04
    - Green 911
    - Red 3685
    - White 27
    - Yellow 729

- Thread for finishing
    - DMC pearl cotton 5, white

- Embroidery needle, size 6
- Dressmakers carbon paper for tracing
- Pencil
- Scissors

PREPARATION

Transfer the design onto the linen fabric
(see page 14). Centre the hoop over the
design, assembling it securely (see page 15).

STITCHES USED

See embroidery stitches on pages 18–23

- Straight stitch
- Back stitch

METHOD

Use two strands of floss. Work all the
embroidery first following the photo. Sew
on the buttons using two strands of floss and
following the photo for placement.

FINISHING

See instructions on page 16 for finishing your
project and attaching the felt backing.

Back stitch 04
(2 strands)

Straight stitch 729
(3 strands)

¼in (6mm) button,
sewn on with 911
(2 strands)

⅛ (3mm) button,
sewn on with 27
(2 strands)

Back stitch 3685
(2 strands)

¼in (6mm) button,
sewn on with 3685
(2 strands)

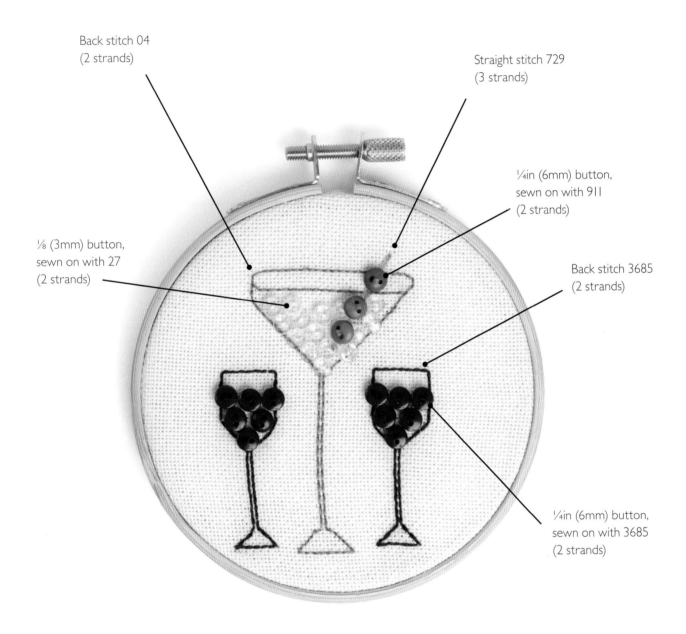

ARTIST'S PALETTE

Simple to create, these large brightly coloured buttons emulate paint. Felt is used to create the palette, and back stitch and satin stitch are used for the brush. This is a perfect gift for an artist friend.

SKILL LEVEL: MEDIUM

YOU'LL NEED

FABRIC
- 10in (25cm) square of ecru linen
- 5in (12.5cm) square of white felt for palette
- 5¾in (14.5cm) circle of white felt for backing

HOOP
- 6in (15cm) embroidery hoop

HABERDASHERY
- Buttons (7)
    Red button, size ⅞in (23mm)
    Orange button, size ⅞in (23mm)
    Yellow button, size ⅞in (23mm)
    Green button, size ⅞in (23mm)
    Blue button, size ⅞in (23mm)
    Purple button, size ⅞in (23mm)
    White button, size ⅞in (23mm)

- Thread
    DMC embroidery floss, 1 skein each:
    Red 666
    Orange 741
    Yellow 17
    Green 702
    Blue 798
    Purple 554
    White 27

    DMC pearl cotton 5:
    Brown 433

- Thread for finishing
    DMC pearl cotton 5, white

- Embroidery needle, size 6

- Dressmakers carbon paper for tracing

- Pencil

- Scissors

PREPARATION

Transfer the design onto the linen fabric (see page 14). Centre the hoop over the design, assembling it securely (see page 15).

STITCHES USED

See embroidery stitches on pages 18–23

- Back stitch
- Satin stitch
- Running stitch

METHOD

Cut out the palette shape (see page 129) in white felt and using tiny running stitches attach it to the background using two strands of white floss, following the photo for placement. Sew on the buttons using two strands of floss in a matching colour, using the photo as a guide. Embroider the paint brush.

FINISHING

See instructions on page 16 for finishing your project and attaching the felt backing.

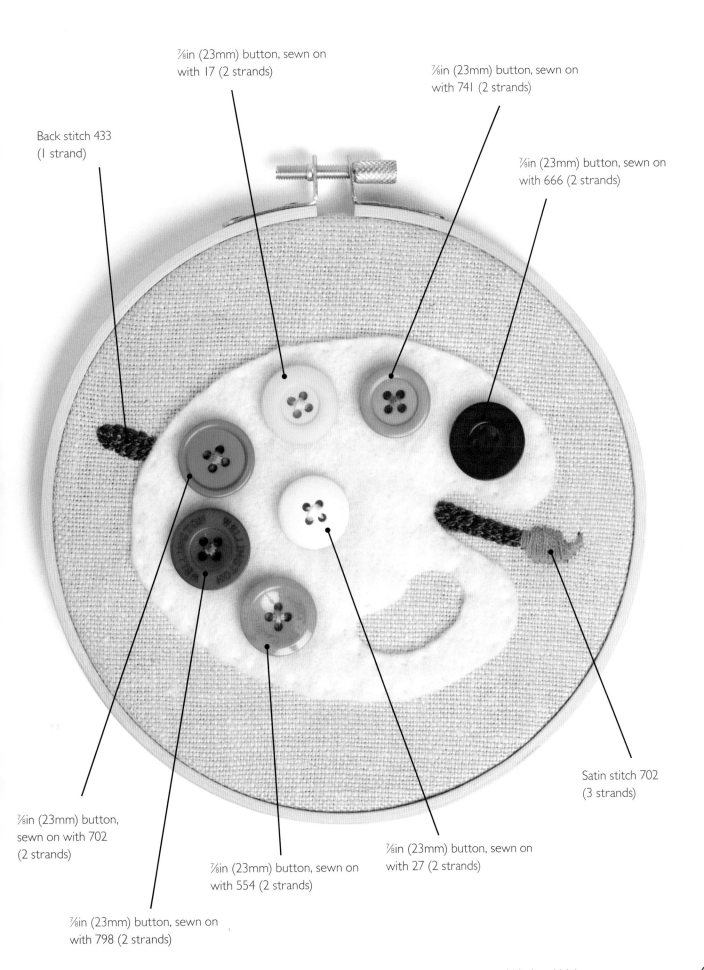

⅞in (23mm) button, sewn on with 17 (2 strands)

⅞in (23mm) button, sewn on with 741 (2 strands)

⅞in (23mm) button, sewn on with 666 (2 strands)

Back stitch 433 (1 strand)

Satin stitch 702 (3 strands)

⅞in (23mm) button, sewn on with 702 (2 strands)

⅞in (23mm) button, sewn on with 554 (2 strands)

⅞in (23mm) button, sewn on with 27 (2 strands)

⅞in (23mm) button, sewn on with 798 (2 strands)

BUTTON JAR

This abstract flower, stitched on felt, makes a perfect topper for a storage jar. This is a great container to hold your favourite buttons, and the top also works as a pin cushion. If your jar has a wider mouth, you will need a larger piece of felt or fabric.

SKILL LEVEL: EASY

YOU'LL NEED

FABRIC
- 8in (20cm) square of white felt (or you could use fabric)

HOOP
- 4in (10cm) embroidery hoop

HABERDASHERY
- Buttons (13)
    1 flower-shaped vintage blue button, size ½in (13mm)
    6 yellow buttons, size ¹¹⁄₃₂in (9mm)
    6 purple buttons, size ¹¹⁄₃₂in (9mm)

- A preserving jar of suitable size such as one with a 3¼in (8.3cm) wide mouth

- Thread
    DMC embroidery floss, 1 skein each:
    Blue 798
    Purple 552
    Yellow 743

    DMC pearl cotton 5:
    Green 699

- Thread for finishing
    DMC pearl cotton 5, white

- Embroidery needle, size 6

- Dressmakers carbon paper for tracing

- Pencil

- Scissors

- Small amount of fibrefill

PREPARATION

Transfer the design onto the felt or fabric (see page 14). Centre the hoop over the design, assembling it securely (see page 15).

STITCHES USED

See embroidery stitches on pages 18–23

- French knot
- Straight stitch

METHOD

Sew on the buttons using two strands of matching floss and following the photo for placement, then work in all the embroidery using the colours shown on the photo.

FINISHING

Press lightly on the wrong side on a padded surface. Using a 7in (17.8cm) plate as a guide, mark a circle centred on the design. Cut around the marked circle. Using pearl cotton, make a running stitch ½in (1.3cm) in from the edge. Gather slightly, insert fibrefill and the flat lid, and pull to gather the fabric tightly, making sure the motif is centred. Fasten the thread securely. Place the cushion on top of the jar and attach using the ring.

French knot 699
(1 strand, wrapped twice)

11/32in (9mm) button, sewn on
with 552 (2 strands)

Straight stitch 699
(1 strand)

French knot 552
(6 strands)

11/32in (9mm) button, sewn on
with 743 (2 strands)

1/2in (13mm) button, sewn on
with 798 (2 strands)

HOLIDAY HOLLY

This felt Christmas ornament also works as a gift tag to add to a holiday present. Simple buttons and easy embroidery make this quick to complete.

SKILL LEVEL: EASY

YOU'LL NEED

FABRIC

- Two 6in (15cm) squares of red felt
- 4in (10cm) square of white felt
- 9in (23cm) length of red rattail cord

HABERDASHERY

- Buttons (6)
  3 red buttons, size ⅜in (10mm)
  3 red buttons, size ⅝₆in (8mm)

- Thread
  DMC embroidery floss, 1 skein each:
  Red 666

  DMC pearl cotton 5:
  Green 367
  Red 666

- Embroidery needle, size 6
- Dressmakers carbon paper for tracing
- Pencil
- Scissors
- Basting thread

PREPARATION

Transfer the design onto the white felt
(see page 14).

STITCHES USED

See embroidery stitches on pages 18–23

- Back stitch

- Blanket stitch

METHOD

Using the template (see page 160) cut out two
larger heart shapes in red. Place the smaller
heart template carefully over the white felt, and
cut it out. Baste the white felt on top of one
of the red hearts. Using one strand of pearl
cotton, work all the embroidery on the two
layered heart following the photo. Sew on the
buttons using two strands of floss and following
the photo for placement.

FINISHING

Remove the basting thread. Make a hanging
loop from the rattail cord and attach it securely
to the top of the plain red heart, using red
thread and running stitch. Layer the two hearts
together so that the embroidery side is on
top and the ends of the loop are concealed.
Stitch together using blanket stitch and red
pearl cotton.

Blanket stitch 666 pearl
cotton (1 strand)

Straight stitch 367
(1 strand)

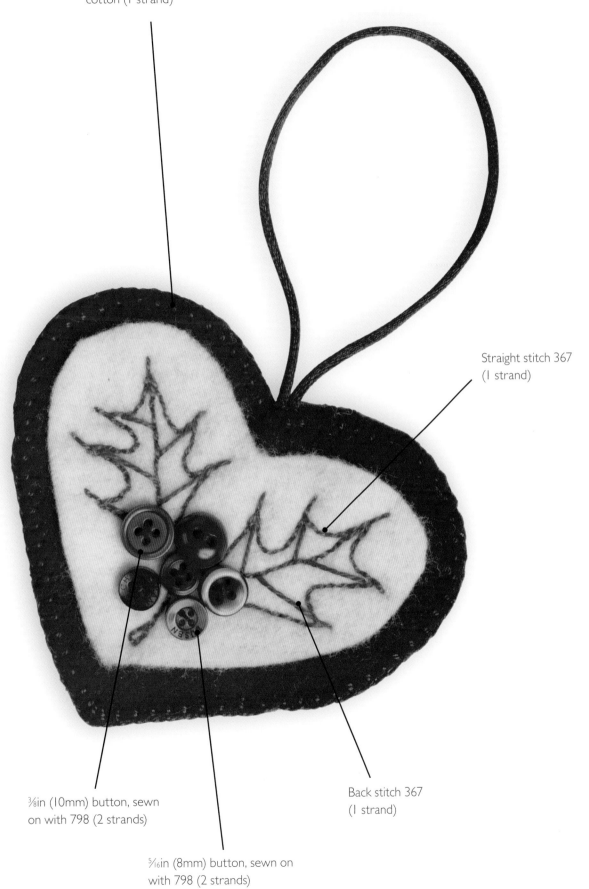

⅜in (10mm) button, sewn
on with 798 (2 strands)

⁵⁄₁₆in (8mm) button, sewn on
with 798 (2 strands)

Back stitch 367
(1 strand)

UNDER THE MISTLETOE

Another quick ornament that is worked on two layers of felt. Hang it from the tree, or use it as a gift tag. These make great gifts and can be personalized with different coloured felt.

SKILL LEVEL: EASY

YOU'LL NEED

FABRIC

- Two 6in (15cm) squares of red felt
- 4in (10cm) square of white felt
- 9in (23cm) length of red rattail cord

HABERDASHERY

- Buttons (11)

    11 white buttons, size $^{11}/_{32}$in (9mm)

- Thread

    DMC embroidery floss, 1 skein each:
    Red 666

    DMC pearl cotton 5:
    Green 367
    Red 666

- Embroidery needle, size 5
- Dressmakers carbon paper for tracing
- Pencil
- Scissors
- Basting thread

PREPARATION
Transfer the design onto the felt (see page 14).

STITCHES USED
See embroidery stitches on pages 18–23

- Back stitch
- Single chain stitch

METHOD
Using the template (see page 160) cut out two larger heart shapes in red and a smaller one in white felt, making sure the template is placed carefully over the design on the white felt. Baste the white felt on top of one of the red hearts. Using one strand of pearl cotton, work all the embroidery on the white heart following the photo. Sew on the buttons using two strands of red floss and following the photo for placement.

FINISHING
Remove the basting thread. Make a hanging loop from the rattail cord and attach it securely to the top of the plain red heart, using red thread and running stitch. Layer the two red hearts together so that the embroidery side on is top and the ends of the loop are concealed. Stitch together using blanket stitch and two strands of red floss.

Blanket stitch 666 pearl
cotton (1 strand)

Back stitch 367 pearl cotton
(1 strand)

Single chain stitch 367
pearl cotton (1 strand)

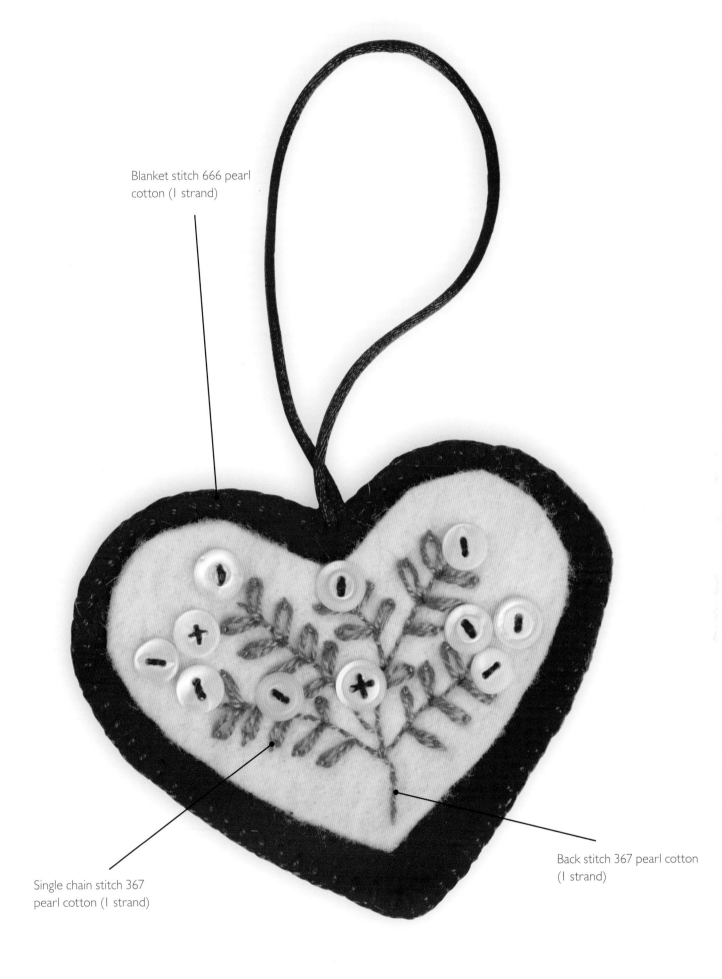

HOLLY BERRY WREATH

Dainty red buttons ring a green centre button on a felt background. Embroidered holly leaves add a touch of whimsy. Perfect for hanging from the tree or door handle.

SKILL LEVEL: EASY

YOU'LL NEED

FABRIC
- Two 6in (15cm) squares of red felt
- 4in (10cm) square of white felt
- ¾yd (70cm) length of red satin ribbon, ¼in (6mm) wide

HOOP
- 5in (13 cm) embroidery hoop (optional)

HABERDASHERY
- Buttons (22)
    1 large green button, size ⅝in (16mm)
    1 large red button, size ½in (13mm)
    2 medium red button, size ⅜in (10mm)
    18 small red buttons, size ⅜in (9mm)

- Thread
    DMC embroidery floss, 1 skein each:
    Red 666

    DMC pearl cotton 5:
    Dark green 367
    Red 666

- Embroidery needle, size 6
- Dressmakers carbon paper for tracing
- Pencil
- Scissors

PREPARATION

Cut a 2½in (6cm) circle of white felt. Baste to the centre of one piece of red felt. Transfer the design onto the felt (see page 14). Centre the hoop over the design, assembling it securely (see page 15).

STITCHES USED

See embroidery stitches on pages 18–23

- French knot
- Single chain stitch
- Straight stitch

METHOD

Sew on the buttons using two strands of floss and following the photo for placement. Using one strand of pearl cotton, work all the embroidery following the photo.

FINISHING

Remove the square from the hoop. Centring the white circle, baste a line around to create a 3in (7.5cm) square. Cut out around the basting line. Cut a second square the same size. Cut 8in (20cm) of ribbon and fold in half for the hanger, and attach it securely to one corner of the plain red square, using red thread and running stitch. Layer the two squares together so that the embroidery side is on top and the ends of the loop are concealed. Stitch together using blanket stitch and red pearl cotton. Tie the remaining ribbon into a bow and slip stitch in place.

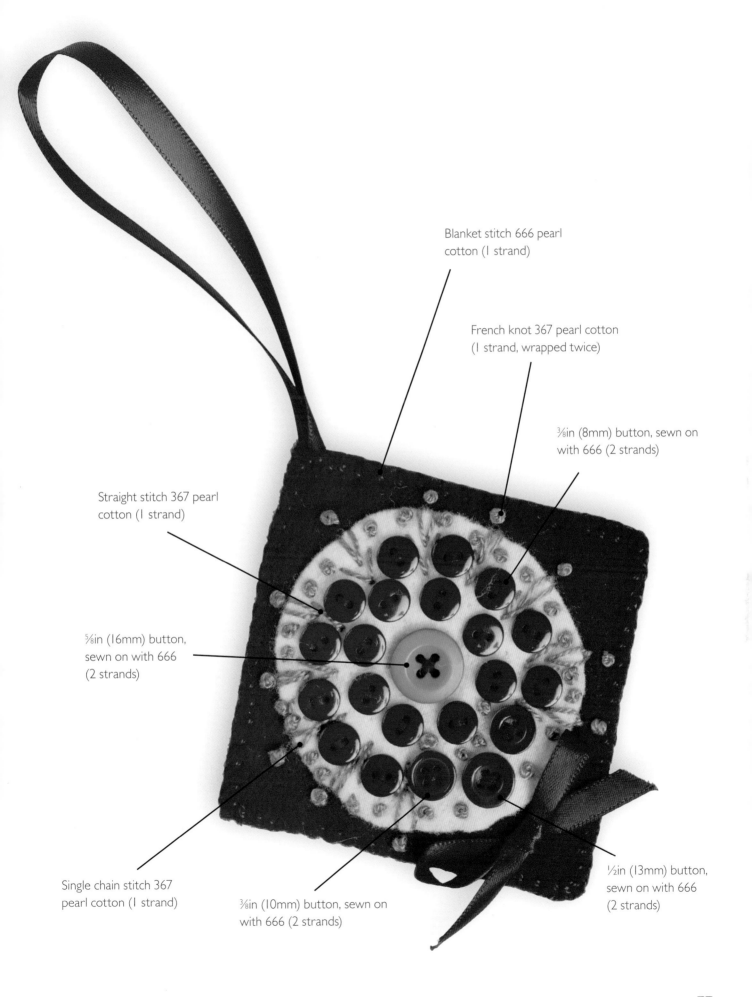

Blanket stitch 666 pearl cotton (1 strand)

French knot 367 pearl cotton (1 strand, wrapped twice)

³⁄₈in (8mm) button, sewn on with 666 (2 strands)

Straight stitch 367 pearl cotton (1 strand)

⁵⁄₈in (16mm) button, sewn on with 666 (2 strands)

Single chain stitch 367 pearl cotton (1 strand)

³⁄₈in (10mm) button, sewn on with 666 (2 strands)

½in (13mm) button, sewn on with 666 (2 strands)

FELT FLOWER NEEDLE CASE

This handy felt needle case is the perfect place to store your sewing and embroidery needles.

SKILL LEVEL: SOME EXPERIENCE

YOU'LL NEED

FABRIC

- Two 9in (23cm) squares of blue felt
- 3½ x 5in (9 x 12.5cm) piece of white felt
- 2in (5cm) square of purple felt
- ¾ yd (0.7m) length of blue satin ribbon, ½in (1.3cm) wide

HOOP

- 7in (18cm) embroidery hoop (optional)

HABERDASHERY

- Buttons (7)

    1 large yellow button, size ⅝in (16mm)

    6 small turquoise buttons, size ¼in (6mm)

- Thread

    DMC embroidery floss, 1 skein each:

    Purple 552

    Yellow 743

    DMC pearl cotton 5:

    Blue 519

    Green 911

    Purple 552

    Yellow 743

- Embroidery needle, size 6
- Dressmakers carbon paper for tracing
- Pencil
- Scissors
- Sewing thread

PREPARATION

Baste a 6½ x 4 ½in (16.5 x 11.5cm) rectangle in the middle of one of the blue pieces of felt. This is the finished size of the needle case. Transfer the design onto one piece of blue felt (see page 14), making sure you centre it on the right-hand half of the rectangle, which will be the front when the cover is folded. Use the photo as a guide. Centre the hoop over the design, assembling it securely (see page 15).

STITCHES USED

See embroidery stitches on pages 18–23

- Back stitch
- French knot
- Single chain stitch
- Straight stitch

METHOD

Cut out the flower shape (see page 161) in the purple felt and baste to the blue felt following the photo. Work the yellow straight stitches. Sew the yellow button on to the centre using two strands of yellow floss. Sew on the tiny turquoise buttons using two strands of purple floss.

Using one strand of pearl cotton, work the embroidery following the photo.

FINISHING

Cut another 6½ x 4 ½in (16.5 x 11.5cm) rectangle to line your case cover. Centre the piece of white felt on the lining and baste in place. Using small running stitches, sew down the centre to attach to the blue felt.

Turn the lining over, so that the white piece is underneath. Cut the ribbon in half and attach one piece to each of the short edges of the lining using small stitches, making sure your work is as neat as possible on the side with the white felt.

Place the embroidered piece and the lining together with the wrong sides facing and using blanket stitch, join the two pieces together.

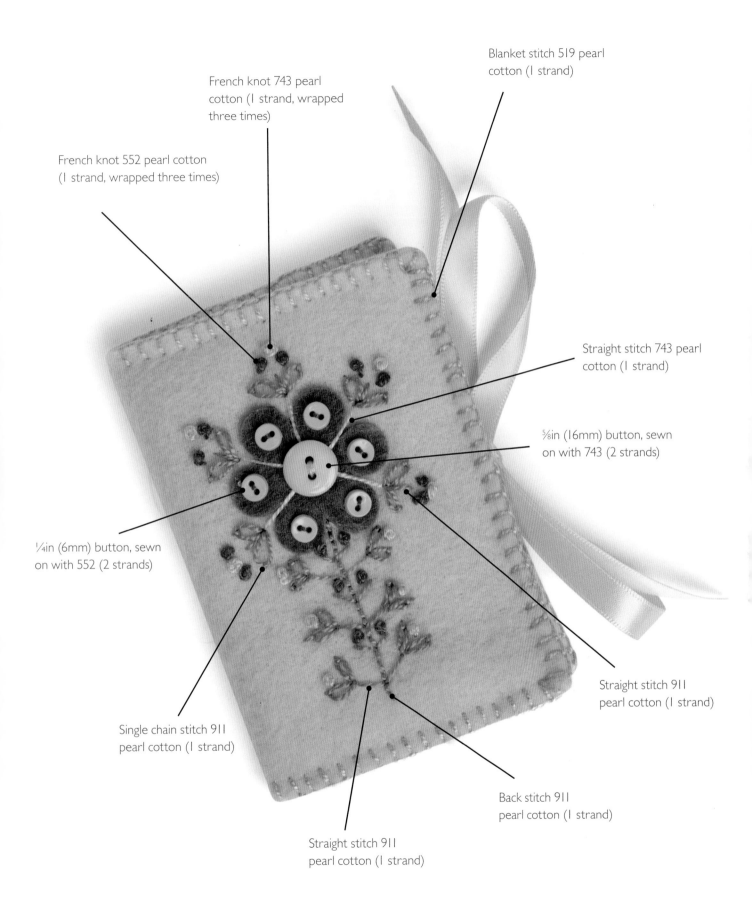

French knot 552 pearl cotton
(1 strand, wrapped three times)

French knot 743 pearl
cotton (1 strand, wrapped
three times)

Blanket stitch 519 pearl
cotton (1 strand)

Straight stitch 743 pearl
cotton (1 strand)

⅝in (16mm) button, sewn
on with 743 (2 strands)

¼in (6mm) button, sewn
on with 552 (2 strands)

Single chain stitch 911
pearl cotton (1 strand)

Straight stitch 911
pearl cotton (1 strand)

Straight stitch 911
pearl cotton (1 strand)

Back stitch 911
pearl cotton (1 strand)

FELT PINCUSHION

Felt is easy to embroider on since the edges don't need finishing, and it can be cut into any shape. This simple pincushion is built from layers of felt, with buttons and embroidery added.

SKILL LEVEL: EASY

YOU'LL NEED

FABRIC

- Two 6in (15cm) squares of light blue felt
- 3in (7.5cm) square of peacock blue felt
- 3in (7.5cm) square of purple felt

HOOP

- 4in (10cm) embroidery hoop

HABERDASHERY

- Buttons (13)

    1 large yellow button, size ¾in (19mm)

    6 medium purple buttons, size ⅝in (15mm)

    6 small turquoise buttons, size ¼in (6mm)

- Thread
    DMC embroidery floss, 1 skein each:
    Purple 552
    Yellow 743

    DMC pearl cotton 5:
    Green 911
    Purple 552
    Yellow 743

- Dressmakers carbon paper for tracing
- Pencil
- Scissors
- Basting thread
- Small amount of fibrefill

- Embroidery needle, size 6

PREPARATION

Transfer the design onto a piece of light blue felt (see page 14). Centre the hoop over the design, assembling it securely (see page 15).

STITCHES USED

See embroidery stitches on pages 18–23

- French knot
- Single chain stitch
- Straight stitch
- Blanket stitch

METHOD

Cut a 1¾in (4.5cm) circle in the peacock blue felt and a flower shape in the purple felt (See the needle case on page 78). Centre both shapes onto the blue felt and baste in place (see photo). Next embroider the straight yellow lines. Attach the purple buttons, using two strands of yellow. Then sew the large yellow button onto the centre of the flower using two strands of floss, then sew the small turquoise buttons onto the flower petals. Lastly embroider the green single chain stitches, and the purple and yellow French knots, following the photo.

FINISHING

Remove the hoop. Press lightly on the wrong side on a padded surface. Baste a 4in (10cm) square around the embroidery. Place the other piece of light blue felt over the embroidery, wrong sides together, and machine stitch or use tiny back stitch (see page 18) to sew together, using the basted square as a guide, and leaving a 2in (5cm) gap in one side. Remove basting thread and trim excess fabric to ½in (1.3cm). Trim across corners, turn the piece to right side, insert fibrefill and hand sew opening closed.

French knot 552 pearl
cotton (1 strand, wrapped
three times)

French knot 743 pearl
cotton (1 strand, wrapped
three times)

¾in (19mm) button, sewn
on with 743 (2 strands)

⅝in (16mm) button, sewn
on with 743 (2 strands)

¼in (6mm) button, sewn
on with 552 (2 strands)

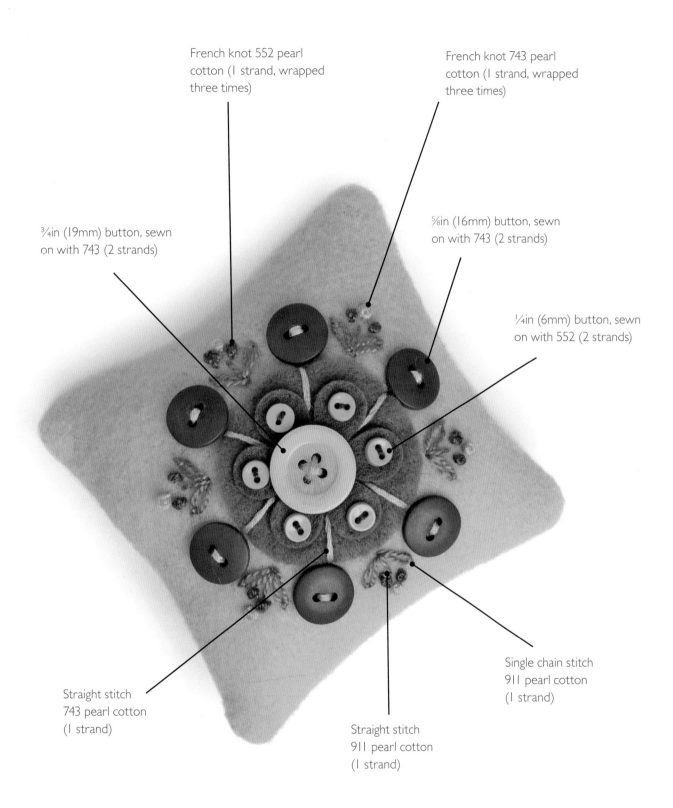

Single chain stitch
911 pearl cotton
(1 strand)

Straight stitch
743 pearl cotton
(1 strand)

Straight stitch
911 pearl cotton
(1 strand)

FORGET-ME-NOT SACHET

I chose to decorate this sachet with blue flowers, which would also look beautiful sewn on a pocket of a pair of jeans or an apron pocket for your gardening friend.

SKILL LEVEL: SOME EXPERIENCE

YOU'LL NEED

FABRIC
- Two 8in (20cm) squares of white linen
- Two 6in (15cm) squares of white cotton for lavender bag
- Approx ¾yd (0.7m) blue satin ribbon, ½in (1.3cm) wide

HOOP
- 4in (10cm) embroidery hoop

HABERDASHERY
- Buttons (25)

    2 blue buttons, size ½in (13mm)

    7 blue buttons, size ⅜in (9mm)

    10 white buttons, size ⅜in (8mm)

    5 dark blue buttons, size ¼in (6mm)

- Thread
  DMC embroidery floss, 1 skein each:
  Green 702
  White 27

- Embroidery needle, size 6
- Dressmakers carbon paper for tracing
- Pencil
- Scissors
- Small amount of dried lavender
- Basting thread
- Sewing thread

PREPARATION

Transfer the design onto the one of the squares of linen fabric (see page 14). Centre the hoop over the design, assembling it securely (see page 15).

STITCHES USED

See embroidery stitches on pages 18–23

- Back stitch
- Single chain stitch

METHOD

Using two or three strands of floss work all the embroidery first following the photo. Work the stems then the leaves. Sew on the buttons using two strands of floss and following the photo for placement.

FINISHING

Remove from hoop, press lightly on the wrong side on a padded surface. Using small running stitches, baste a rectangle 4 x 5¾in (10 x 14.5cm) around the embroidery, basting the lower line ½in (1.3cm) away from the flower stem. This represents the finished size.

Place the stitched piece on top of the unstitched piece of linen with right sides together. Following the basting lines on the finished piece, baste the two pieces together on three sides. Machine or back stitch (see page 18) along the basting lines, leaving the top open. Trim excess fabric away to ½in (1.3cm) from the seams, except for the top. Trim across the bottom corners, turn the piece to the right side, and square out the corners. Fold in approximately 1in (2.5cm) hem at the top and sew in place.

Using cotton fabric, make a lining bag approximately 3¼ x 4 ¼in (8 x 11cm). Fill the bag with lavender and sew the top closed. Insert inside the linen embroidery and tie the ribbon in a bow around the top.

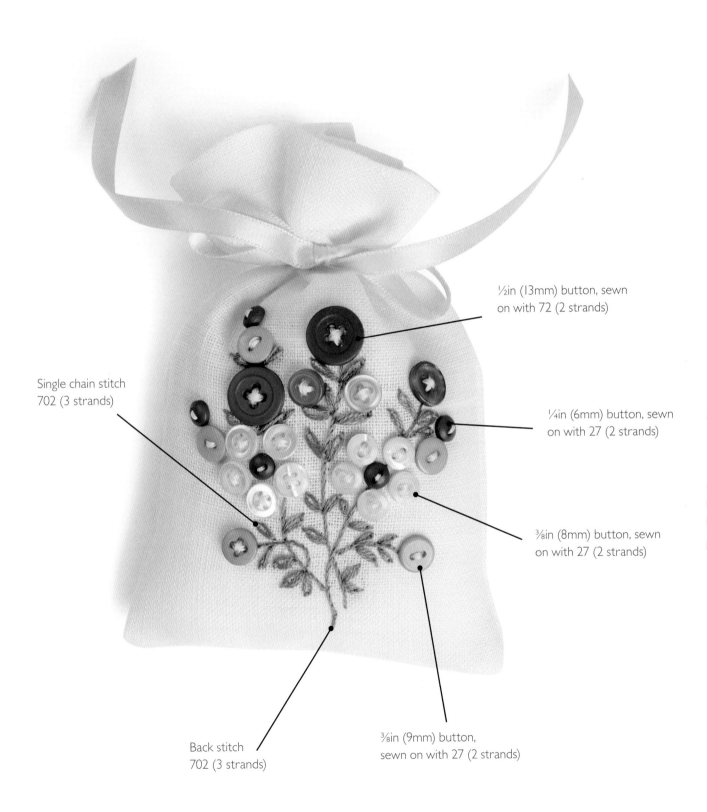

½in (13mm) button, sewn
on with 72 (2 strands)

Single chain stitch
702 (3 strands)

¼in (6mm) button, sewn
on with 27 (2 strands)

⅜in (8mm) button, sewn
on with 27 (2 strands)

Back stitch
702 (3 strands)

⅜in (9mm) button,
sewn on with 27 (2 strands)

GOLDEN YARROW FLOWER SACHET

This flower, according to folklore, helps people find their sweetheart. Hang this lovely sachet, filled with lavender, in your closet or on the door to keep your clothes smelling fresh.

SKILL LEVEL: SOME EXPERIENCE

YOU'LL NEED

FABRIC
- Two 8in (20cm) squares of white linen
- Approx 1yd (1m) of white satin ribbon, ½in (13mm) wide

HOOP
- 4in (10cm) embroidery hoop

HABERDASHERY
- Buttons (20)
    14 yellow buttons, size ⅜in (9mm)
    6 orange buttons, size ⅜in (9mm)

- Thread
    DMC embroidery floss, 1 skein each:
    Orange 9741
    Yellow 742

    DMC Pearl Cotton 5:
    Green 702

- Embroidery needle, size 6
- Dressmakers carbon paper for tracing
- Pencil
- Scissors
- Small amount of fibrefill, lavender or potpourri
- Basting thread
- Sewing thread

PREPARATION

Transfer the design onto one piece of linen fabric (see page 14). Centre the hoop over the design, assembling it securely (see page 15).

STITCHES USED

See embroidery stitches on pages 18–23

- Back stitch
- French knot
- Straight stitch

METHOD

Using one strand of pearl cotton, work the stems and leaves. Using three strands of floss, work the French knots. Sew on the buttons using two strands of floss and following the photo for placement.

FINISHING

Remove from the hoop and press lightly on the wrong side on a padded surface. Using small running stitches, baste a rectangle 3¾ × 5¼in (9.5 × 13.3cm) around the embroidery, basting the lower line ½in (1.3cm) away from the flower stem.

Place the stitched piece on top of the unstitched piece of linen with right sides together. Following the basting lines on the finished piece, baste the two pieces together on three sides, leaving the top open. Machine or hand stitch along the basting lines. Trim excess fabric to ½in (1.3cm) from the seams; leave approx ¾in (1.9cm) above the basting line at the top edge. Trim across the bottom corners, turn to the right side, square out the corners and press. Stuff with fibrefill, lavender or a potpourri sachet.

Press the seam allowance to the inside at the top and sew closed along the basting line. Tie a bow at one end of the ribbon, secure the other end of the ribbon to the back of the bow to from a loop, and then sew it to the centre of the sachet.

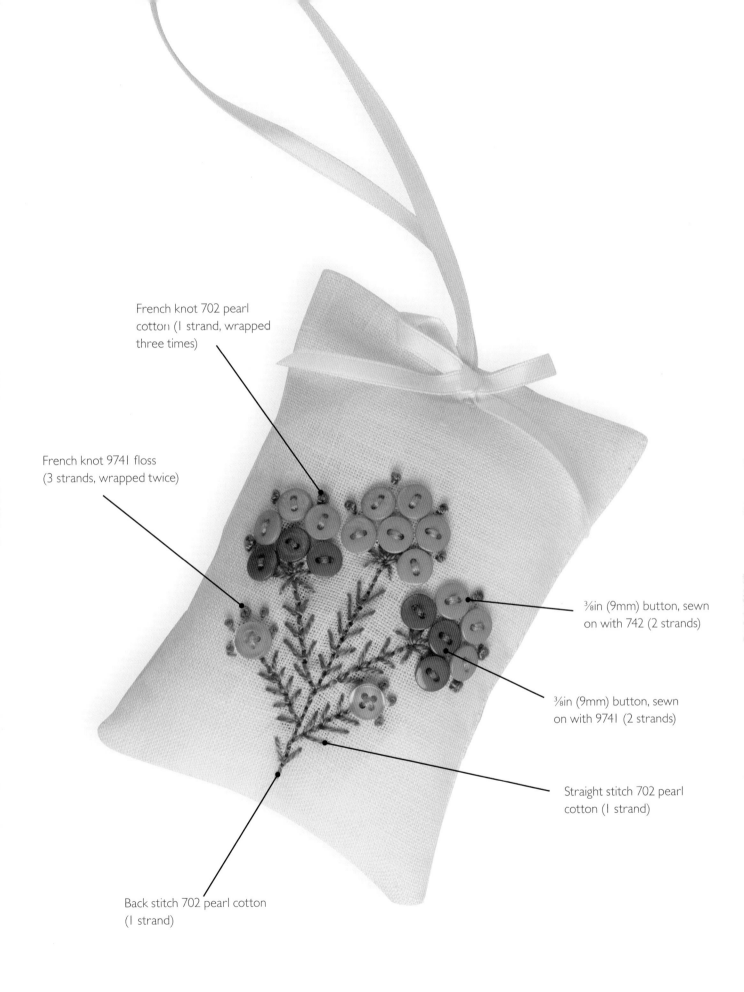

French knot 702 pearl
cotton (1 strand, wrapped
three times)

French knot 9741 floss
(3 strands, wrapped twice)

⅜in (9mm) button, sewn
on with 742 (2 strands)

⅜in (9mm) button, sewn
on with 9741 (2 strands)

Straight stitch 702 pearl
cotton (1 strand)

Back stitch 702 pearl cotton
(1 strand)

APPLE TREE

I dug through my button collection for a selection of red buttons to create apples. Simple back stitch is used to outline the tree, and single chain stitches make the leaves.

SKILL LEVEL: MEDIUM

YOU'LL NEED

FABRIC
- 12in (30cm) square of green linen
- 7¾in (19.5cm) circle of white felt for backing

HOOP
- 8in (20cm) embroidery hoop

HABERDASHERY
- Buttons (19)

    4 red buttons, size ⅝in (16mm)

    1 red button, size ½in (13mm)

    10 red buttons, size ⅜in (10mm)

    4 buttons, size ⁵⁄₁₆in (8mm)

- Thread
    DMC embroidery floss, 1 skein each:
    Red 666

    DMC pearl cotton 5:
    Brown 433
    Dark green 699
    Light green 702

- Thread for finishing:
    DMC pearl cotton 5, white

- Embroidery needle, size 6

- Dressmakers carbon paper for tracing

- Pencil

- Scissors

PREPARATION

Transfer the design onto the fabric (see page 14). Centre the hoop over the design, assembling it securely (see page 15).

STITCHES USED

See embroidery stitches on pages 18–23

- Back stitch
- Single chain stitch

METHOD

Use one strand of pearl cotton and back stitch to work the tree trunk first, then work the leaves and the grass. Sew on the buttons using two strands of floss and following the photo for placement.

FINISHING

See instructions on page 16 for finishing your project and attaching the felt backing.

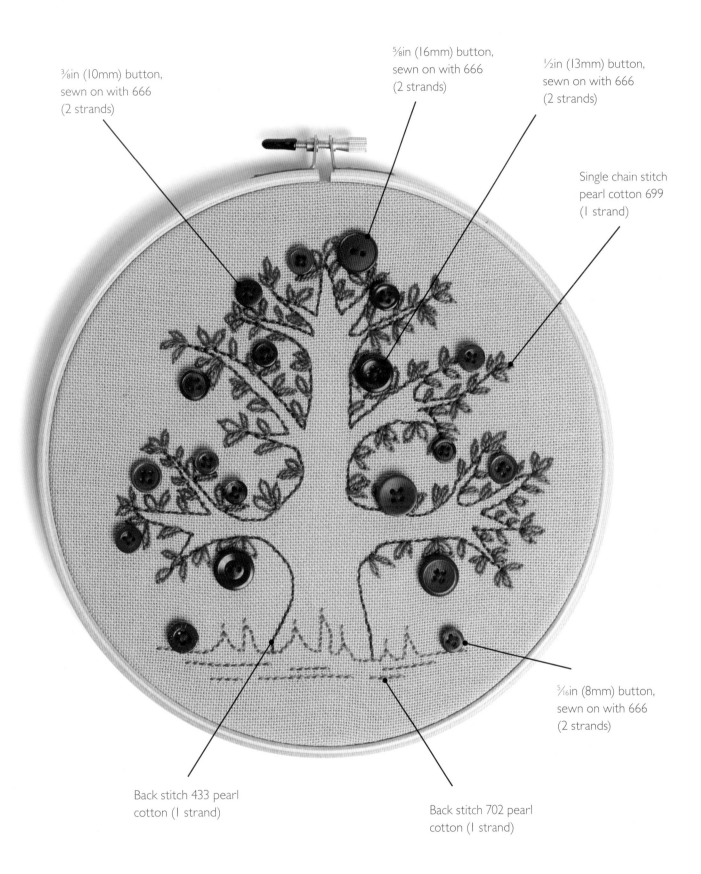

⅜in (10mm) button, sewn on with 666 (2 strands)

⅝in (16mm) button, sewn on with 666 (2 strands)

½in (13mm) button, sewn on with 666 (2 strands)

Single chain stitch pearl cotton 699 (1 strand)

Back stitch 433 pearl cotton (1 strand)

Back stitch 702 pearl cotton (1 strand)

⁵⁄₁₆in (8mm) button, sewn on with 666 (2 strands)

GREEN PEPPER NAPKIN

This makes a very special housewarming gift! Back stitch and French knots are worked in pearl cotton, buttons are stitched on for the seeds. This motif would be charming worked in a row on a tea towel, with a selection of red, yellow and green peppers.

SKILL LEVEL: EASY

YOU'LL NEED

FABRIC
- 20in (50cm) square green napkin
  (or similar size)

HOOP
- 4in (10cm) embroidery hoop

HABERDASHERY
- Buttons (16)
  16 small pale yellow buttons, size ¼in (6mm)

- Thread
  DMC embroidery floss, 1 skein each:
  Yellow 745

  DMC Pearl Cotton 5:
  Green 702
  White

- Embroidery needle, size 6

- Dressmakers carbon paper for tracing

- Pencil

- Scissors

PREPARATION

Transfer the design (see page 14) onto
the corner of the napkin, see photo. Centre
the hoop over the design, assembling it
securely (see page 15).

STITCHES USED

See embroidery stitches on pages 18–23

- French knot

- Back stitch

METHOD

Using one strand of pearl cotton, work the back
stitch first, then the French knots. Sew on the
buttons using two strands of floss and following
the photo for placement.

FINISHING

Remove the hoop. Press lightly on the wrong
side on a padded surface.

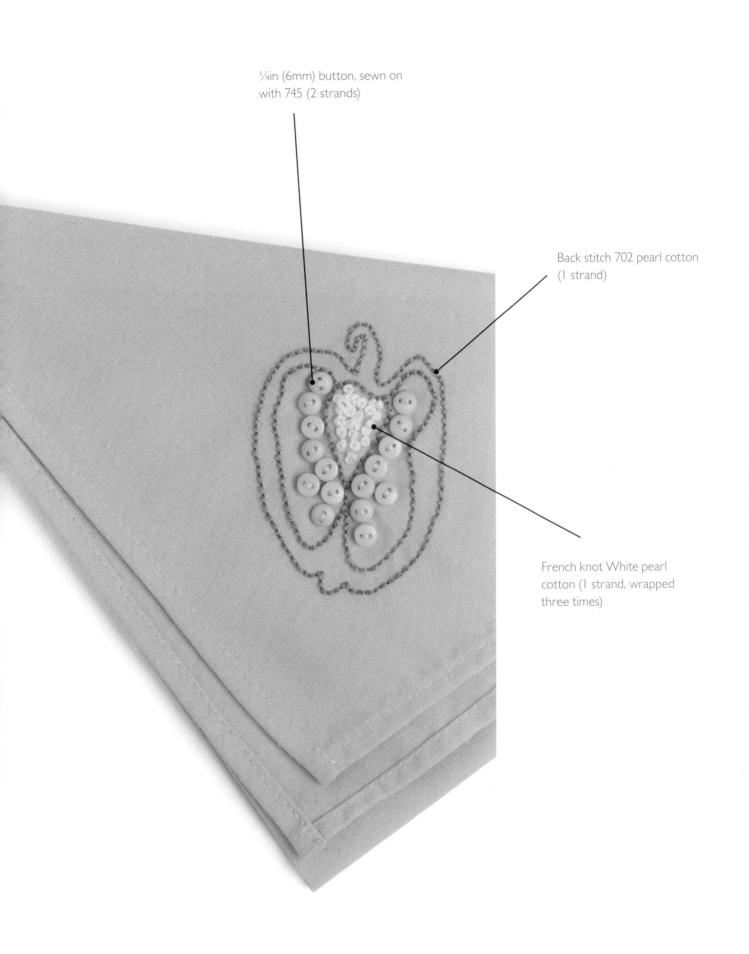

¼in (6mm) button, sewn on
with 745 (2 strands)

Back stitch 702 pearl cotton
(1 strand)

French knot White pearl
cotton (1 strand, wrapped
three times)

PEAPOD NAPKIN

I made a set of four of these embroidered napkins and gave them to my vegetable gardener friend, in exchange for a basket of her garden spoils.

SKILL LEVEL: EASY

YOU'LL NEED

FABRIC
- 20in (50cm) square green napkin (or similar size)

HOOP
- 4in (10cm) embroidery hoop

HABERDASHERY
- Buttons (10)

    3 purple buttons, size $^{11}\!/_{32}$in (9mm)

    3 green buttons, size $^{11}\!/_{32}$in (9mm)

    4 small green buttons, size $^{1}\!/_{4}$in (6mm)

- Thread
    DMC embroidery floss, 1 skein each:
    Green 703
    Purple 552

    DMC pearl cotton 5:
    Light green 702

- Embroidery needle, size 6
- Dressmakers carbon paper for tracing
- Pencil
- Scissors

PREPARATION

Transfer the design (see page 14) onto the corner of the napkin, see photo. Centre the hoop over the design, assembling it securely (see page 15).

STITCHES USED

See embroidery stitches on pages 18–23

- French knot
- Stem stitch
- Back stitch

METHOD

Work all the embroidery first. Sew on the buttons using two strands of floss and following the photo for placement.

FINISHING

Remove the hoop. Press lightly on the wrong side on a padded surface.

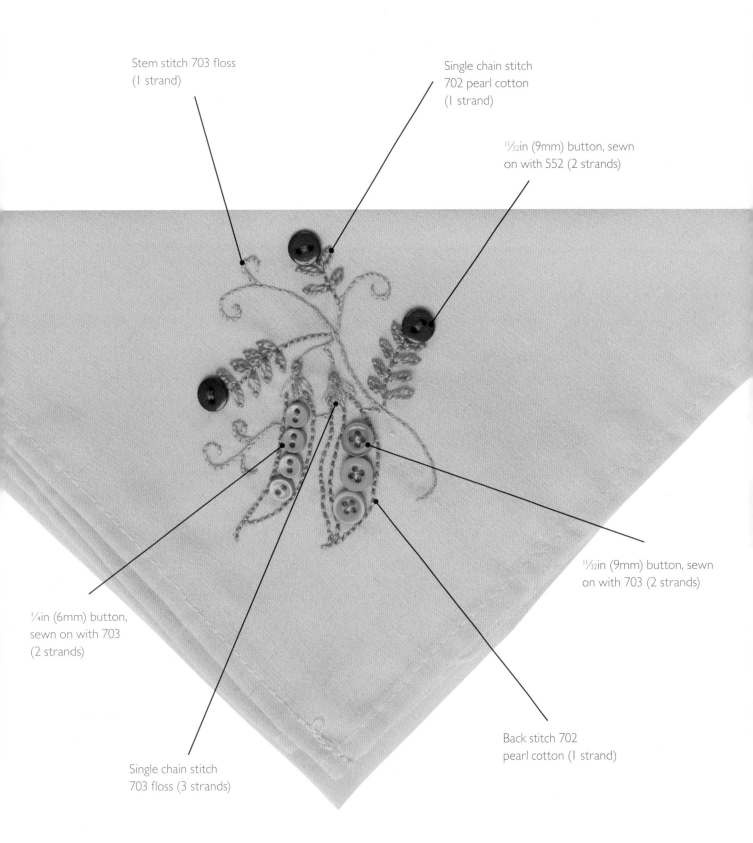

Stem stitch 703 floss
(1 strand)

Single chain stitch
702 pearl cotton
(1 strand)

¹¹⁄₃₂in (9mm) button, sewn
on with 552 (2 strands)

¹¹⁄₃₂in (9mm) button, sewn
on with 703 (2 strands)

¼in (6mm) button,
sewn on with 703
(2 strands)

Single chain stitch
703 floss (3 strands)

Back stitch 702
pearl cotton (1 strand)

CRAB APPLE BLOSSOM NAPKIN

Inspired by a beautiful tree outside my studio, this lovely branch features buttons in varying shades and sizes, as well as delicate leaves worked in fishbone stitch.

SKILL LEVEL: SOME EXPERIENCE

YOU'LL NEED

FABRIC
- 20in (50cm) square white napkin (or similar size)

HOOP
- 4in (10cm) embroidery hoop

HABERDASHERY
- Buttons (12)

    1 dark red button, size ⅝in (16mm)

    1 red button, size ⅝in (16mm)

    2 dark red buttons, size ½in (13mm)

    2 red buttons, size ½in (13mm)

    6 pink buttons, size ¼in (6mm)

- Thread
    DMC embroidery floss, 1 skein each:
    Brown 632
    Green 704
    Red 309

- Embroidery needle, size 6
- Dressmakers carbon paper for tracing
- Pencil
- Scissors

PREPARATION

Transfer the design (see page 14) onto the corner of the napkin, see photo. Centre the hoop over the design, assembling it securely (see page 15).

STITCHES USED

See embroidery stitches on pages 18–23

- Back stitch

- Fishbone stitch

- Single chain stitch

METHOD

Using four and two strands of floss, work all the embroidery first. Sew on the buttons using two strands of floss and following the photo for placement.

FINISHING

Remove the hoop. Press lightly on the wrong side on a padded surface.

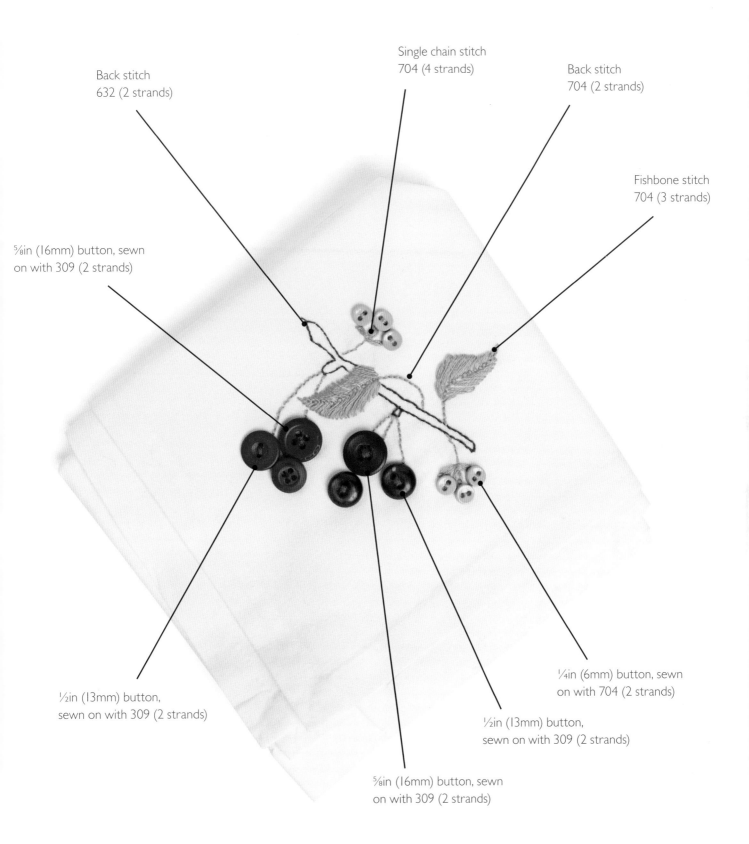

Back stitch
632 (2 strands)

Single chain stitch
704 (4 strands)

Back stitch
704 (2 strands)

Fishbone stitch
704 (3 strands)

⅝in (16mm) button, sewn
on with 309 (2 strands)

½in (13mm) button,
sewn on with 309 (2 strands)

¼in (6mm) button, sewn
on with 704 (2 strands)

½in (13mm) button,
sewn on with 309 (2 strands)

⅝in (16mm) button, sewn
on with 309 (2 strands)

BLUEBERRY NAPKIN

A summer fruit, blueberries grow in abundance in my garden. Here, clusters of berries are intertwined with tiny green leaves. These napkins bring excitement and curiosity to your tablescape.

SKILL LEVEL: SOME EXPERIENCE

YOU'LL NEED

FABRIC
- 20in (50cm) square white napkin (or similar size)

HOOP
- 4in (10cm) embroidery hoop

HABERDASHERY
- Buttons (18)

    1 large blue button, size ½in (13mm)

    13 medium blue buttons, size ⅜in (10mm)

    2 blue buttons, size ¹¹⁄₃₂in (9mm)

    2 blue buttons, size ⁵⁄₁₆in (8mm)

- Thread
    DMC embroidery floss, 1 skein each:
    Blue 798

    DMC pearl cotton 5:
    Light green 702

- Embroidery needle, size 6
- Dressmakers carbon paper for tracing
- Pencil
- Scissors

PREPARATION

Transfer the design (see page 14) onto the corner of the napkin, see photo. Centre the hoop over the design, assembling it securely (see page 15).

STITCHES USED

See embroidery stitches on pages 18-23

- Back stitch

- Single chain stitch

- Straight stitch

METHOD

Using one strand of pearl cotton, work all the embroidery first. Sew on the buttons using two strands of floss and following the photo for placement.

FINISHING

Remove the hoop. Press lightly on the wrong side on a padded surface.

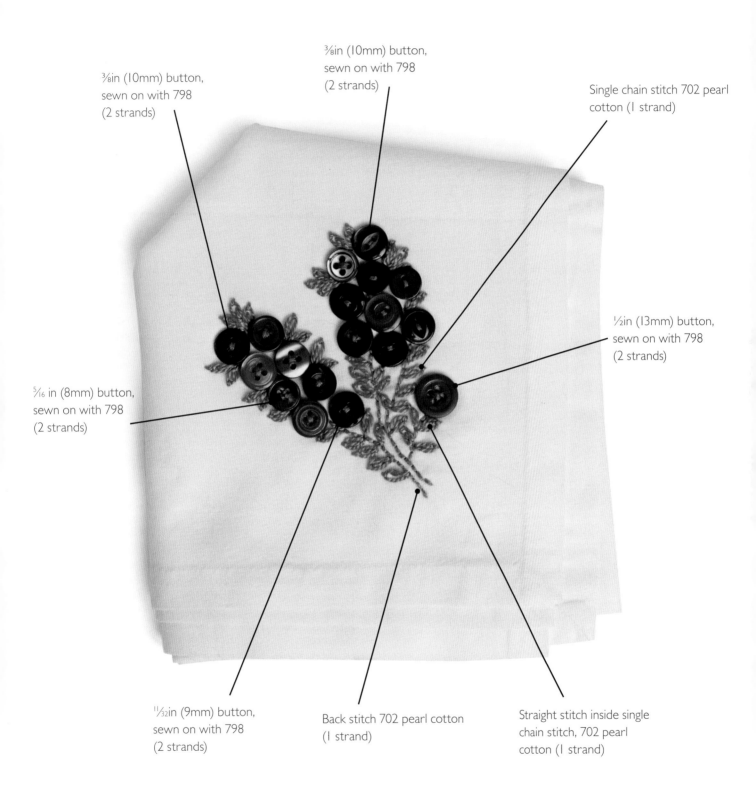

⅜in (10mm) button, sewn on with 798 (2 strands)

⅜in (10mm) button, sewn on with 798 (2 strands)

Single chain stitch 702 pearl cotton (1 strand)

½in (13mm) button, sewn on with 798 (2 strands)

⁵⁄₁₆ in (8mm) button, sewn on with 798 (2 strands)

¹¹⁄₃₂in (9mm) button, sewn on with 798 (2 strands)

Back stitch 702 pearl cotton (1 strand)

Straight stitch inside single chain stitch, 702 pearl cotton (1 strand)

FLORAL WREATH

Raid your button tin for your favourite vintage buttons to create a unique and very special wreath. I chose a blue and green palette, but pinks and peaches would work equally as well with the white buttons.

SKILL LEVEL: SOME EXPERIENCE

YOU'LL NEED

FABRIC
- 12in (30cm) square of white linen
- 7½in (19cm) circle of white felt for backing

HOOP
- 8in (20cm) embroidery hoop

HABERDASHERY
- Buttons (60)

    7 white/mother-of-pearl buttons, size 1in (25mm)

    6 blue buttons, size ½in (13mm)

    25 assorted white/blue/green buttons, size ⅜in (10mm)

    22 assorted white/blue/green buttons, size ⁵⁄₁₆in (8mm)

- Thread
    DMC embroidery floss, 1 skein each:
    Blue 826
    Green 3346

- Thread for finishing
    DMC pearl cotton 5, white

- Embroidery needle, size 6

- Dressmakers carbon paper for tracing

- Pencil

- Scissors

PREPARATION

Transfer the design onto the linen fabric (see page 14). Centre the hoop over the design, assembling it securely (see page 15).

STITCHES USED

See embroidery stitches on pages 18–23

- French knot
- Single chain
- Fly stitch

METHOD

Sew on the buttons using two strands of floss and following the photo for placement. Using three strands of floss for all embroidery, except the French knots which need six strands, work embroidery last.

FINISHING

See instructions on page 16 for finishing your project and attaching the felt backing.

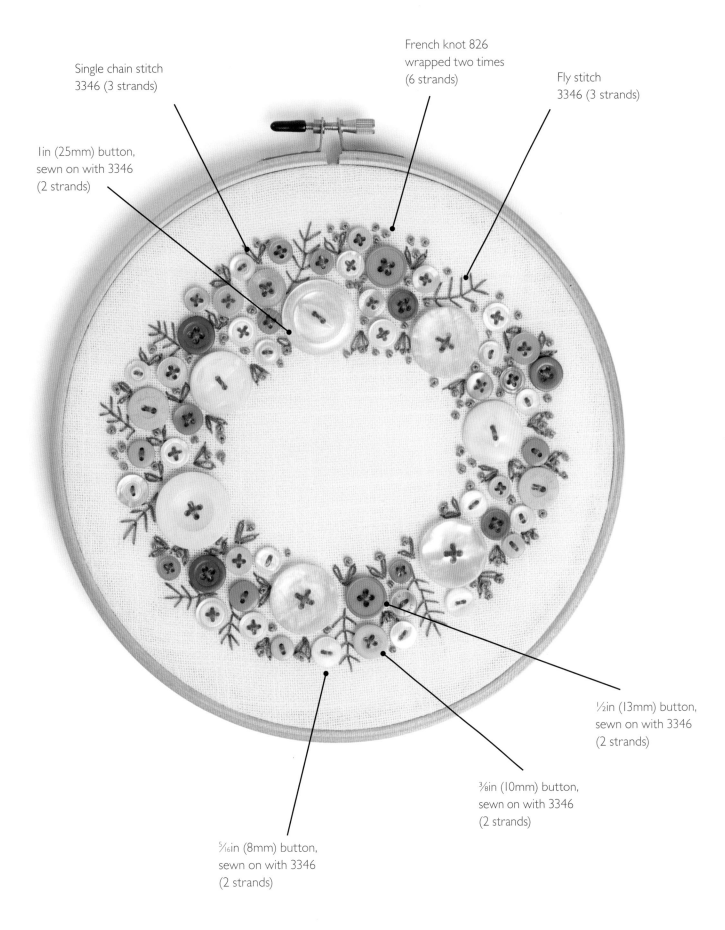

Single chain stitch
3346 (3 strands)

French knot 826
wrapped two times
(6 strands)

Fly stitch
3346 (3 strands)

1in (25mm) button,
sewn on with 3346
(2 strands)

½in (13mm) button,
sewn on with 3346
(2 strands)

⅜in (10mm) button,
sewn on with 3346
(2 strands)

⁵⁄₁₆in (8mm) button,
sewn on with 3346
(2 strands)

BOUQUET OF FLOWERS

Select an array of coloured buttons and styles to create this beautiful bouquet. It will be equally beautiful using all white buttons on an oatmeal background, or a multicoloured mix on white. Change the ribbon colour to suit.

SKILL LEVEL: SOME EXPERIENCE

YOU'LL NEED

FABRIC
- 12in (30cm) square of white linen
- 7½in (19cm) circle of white felt for backing
- ¾ yd (0.7m) length of yellow satin ribbon, ⅝in (16mm) wide

HOOP
- 8in (20cm) embroidery hoop

HABERDASHERY
- Buttons (84)

    7 assorted buttons, size ¾in (19mm)

    4 assorted buttons, size ½in (13mm)

    23 assorted buttons, size ⅜in (10mm)

    35 assorted buttons, size ⁵⁄₁₆in (8mm)

    15 assorted buttons, size ¼in (6mm)

- Thread
    DMC embroidery floss, 1 skein each:
    Green 911

    DMC pearl cotton 5:
    Green 911

- Thread for finishing
    DMC pearl cotton 5, white

- Embroidery needle, size 6

- Dressmakers carbon paper for tracing

- Pencil

- Scissors

PREPARATION

Transfer the design onto the fabric (see page 14). Centre the hoop over the design, assembling it securely (see page 15).

STITCHES USED

See embroidery stitches on pages 18–23

- Stem stitch

METHOD

Using one strand of pearl cotton, work embroidery first. Sew on the buttons using two strands of floss and following the photo for placement.

FINISHING

Tie the satin ribbon into a bow and fasten to white linen with needle and white thread. See instructions on page 16 for finishing your project and attaching the felt backing.

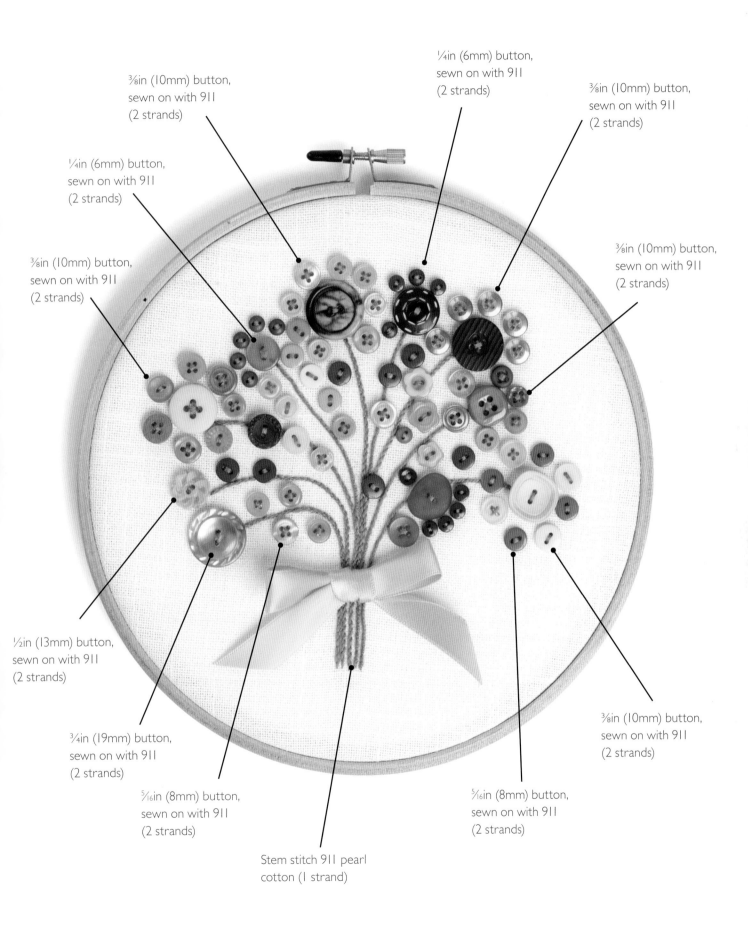

⅜in (10mm) button, sewn on with 911 (2 strands)

¼in (6mm) button, sewn on with 911 (2 strands)

⅜in (10mm) button, sewn on with 911 (2 strands)

¼in (6mm) button, sewn on with 911 (2 strands)

⅜in (10mm) button, sewn on with 911 (2 strands)

⅜in (10mm) button, sewn on with 911 (2 strands)

½in (13mm) button, sewn on with 911 (2 strands)

¾in (19mm) button, sewn on with 911 (2 strands)

⁵⁄₁₆in (8mm) button, sewn on with 911 (2 strands)

Stem stitch 911 pearl cotton (1 strand)

⁵⁄₁₆in (8mm) button, sewn on with 911 (2 strands)

⅜in (10mm) button, sewn on with 911 (2 strands)

AFTERNOON TEA

Being British, I enjoy a relaxing cup of tea in the afternoon. This whimsical teapot is inspired by a collection of blue china from Europe.

SKILL LEVEL: SOME EXPERIENCE

YOU'LL NEED

FABRIC
- 18 x 26in (46 x 66cm) white linen tea towel (or similar size)

HOOP
- 6in (15cm) embroidery hoop

HABERDASHERY
- Buttons (23):

    1 vintage blue button, size ½in (13mm)

    22 blue buttons, size ¼in (6mm)

- Thread
    DMC embroidery floss, 1 skein each:
    White 27

    DMC pearl cotton 5:
    Blue 799

- Embroidery needle, size 6
- Dressmakers carbon paper for tracing
- Pencil
- Scissors

PREPARATION

Transfer the design (see page 14) onto the centre of the tea towel, 2in (5cm) above the hem, see photo. Centre the hoop over the design, assembling it securely (see page 15).

STITCHES USED

See embroidery stitches on pages 18–23

• Back stitch

METHOD

Using one strand of pearl cotton, work all the embroidery first. Sew on the buttons using two strands of floss and following the photo for placement.

FINISHING

Remove the hoop. Press lightly on the wrong side on a padded surface.

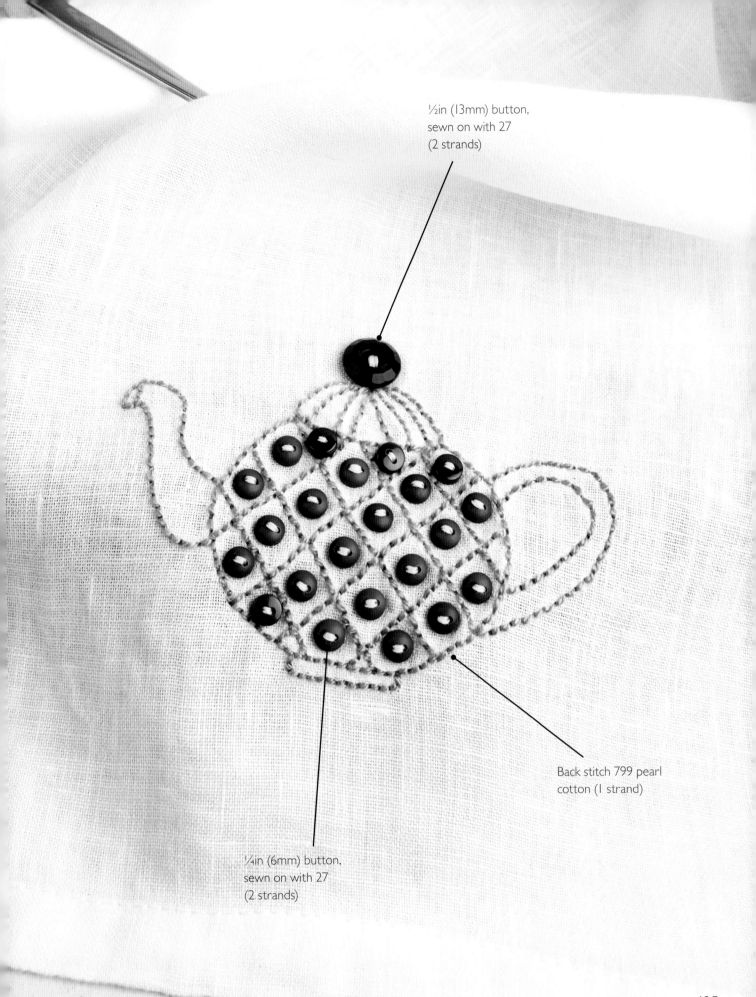

½in (13mm) button,
sewn on with 27
(2 strands)

Back stitch 799 pearl
cotton (1 strand)

¼in (6mm) button,
sewn on with 27
(2 strands)

TEMPLATES

Over the following pages are the templates
required for the projects. All templates are 100%
unless otherwise stated.

MANDALA (PAGE 38)

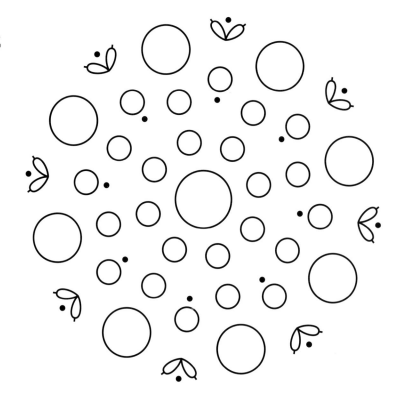

MINI WREATH HOOP (PAGE 26)

SCANDI-INSPIRED FLOWERS
(PAGE 30)

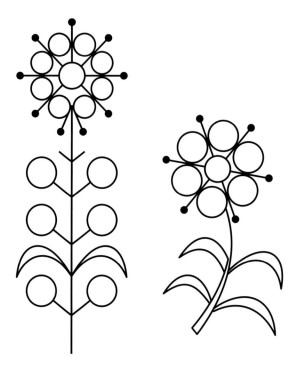

OH, CHRISTMAS TREE (PAGE 34)

MONARCH BUTTERFLY (PAGE 42)

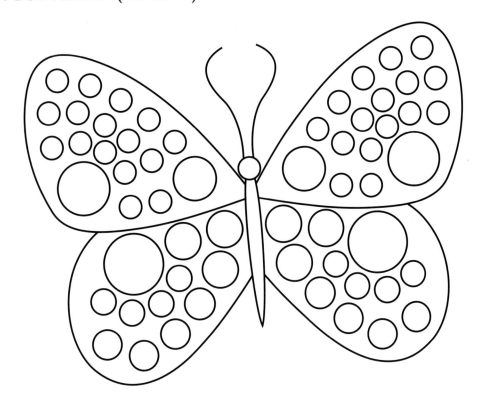

QUEEN ANNE'S LACE (PAGE 46)

FELT MANDALA (PAGE 50)

ARTIST'S PALETTE (PAGE 58)

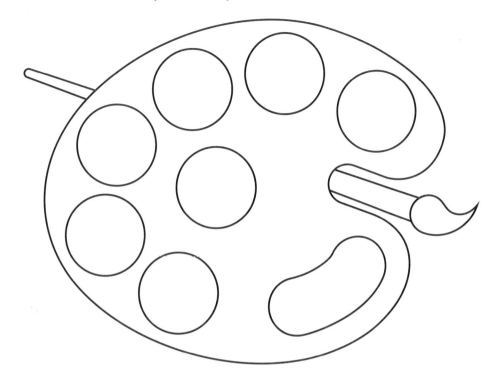

COCKTAIL TIME (PAGE 54)

BUTTON JAR (PAGE 62)

HOLIDAY HOLLY (PAGE 66)

UNDER THE MISTLETOE (PAGE 70)

HOLLY BERRY WREATH (PAGE 74)

FELT FLOWER NEEDLE CASE (PAGE 78)

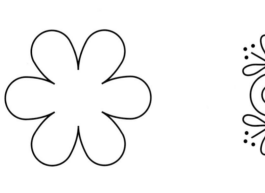

FELT PINCUSHION (PAGE 82)

FORGET-ME-NOT SACHET (PAGE 86)

GOLDEN YARROW FLOWER SACHET (PAGE 90)

APPLE TREE (PAGE 94)

FLORAL WREATH (PAGE 114)

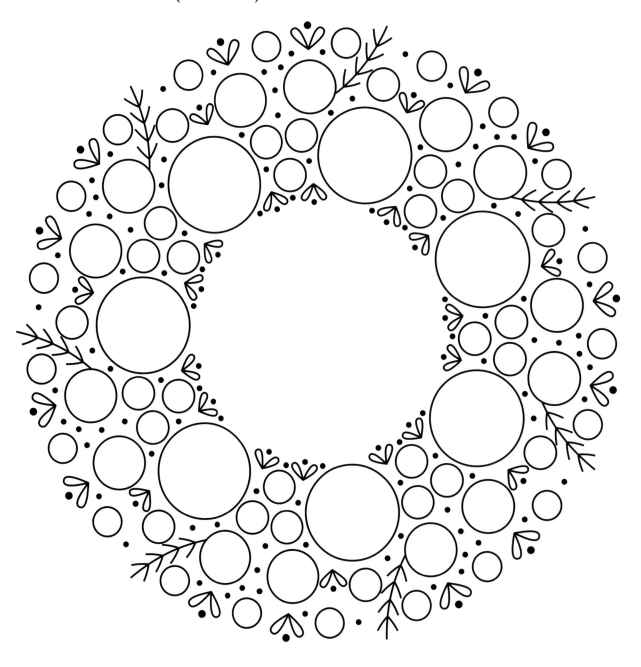

BOUQUET OF FLOWERS (PAGE 118)

GREEN PEPPER NAPKIN (PAGE 98)

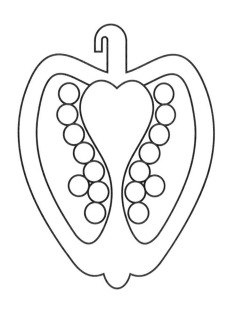

BLUEBERRY NAPKIN (PAGE 110)

PEAPOD NAPKIN (PAGE 102)

CRAB APPLE BLOSSOM NAPKIN
(PAGE 106)

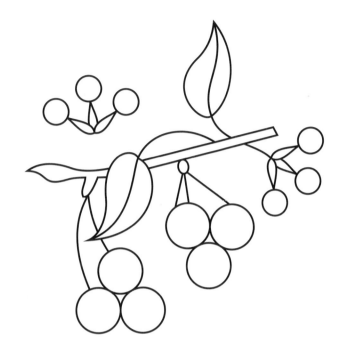

AFTERNOON TEA (PAGE 122)

RESOURCES

Fabric, felt, thread and embroidery hoops:
Amazon – amazon.co.uk
Hobbycraft – hobbycraft.co.uk

Embroidery floss and pearl cotton:
DMC – dmc.com

ACKNOWLEDGEMENTS

I would like to thank the talented staff at Quail Studio for creating such a beautiful book. Special thanks to my friend, Trisha Malcolm, for encouraging me to pick up my embroidery needle again, and thanks to my editor, Karin Strom. I could not have created the embroideries without the support of my family and friends who spurred me on during the good days and through these challenging times. Lastly, I owe all this to a wonderful lady, Joan Toggitt, who guided me on my long and wonderful career in the embroidery world, even long after she had left us. She was, and still is, my guardian angel.

INDEX

To order a book, or to request
a catalogue, contact:

GMC Publications Ltd
Castle Place, 166 High Street,
Lewes, East Sussex,
BN7 1XU
United Kingdom
Tel: +44 (0)1273 488005
www.gmcbooks.com